BERSERK

HAMILCAR NOIR | TRUE CRIME LIBRARY #1

DON STRADLEY

BERSERK

THE SHOCKING LIFE AND DEATH OF EDWIN VALERO

HAMILCAR NOIR

HARD-HITTING TRUE CRIME

ISBN: 978-1-949590-14-2

Publisher's Cataloging-in-Publication Data
Names: Stradley, Don, author.
Title: Berserk: the shocking life and death of Edwin Valero / Don Stradley.
Description: Includes bibliographical references. | Boston, MA: Hamilcar Publications, 2019.
Identifiers: LCCN 2019940887 | ISBN 9781949590142
Subjects: LCSH Valero, Edwin, 1981–2010. | Boxers (Sports)—Biography. | Boxers (Sports)—Venezuela—Biography. | Boxing—Venezuela—History. | Murder—Venezuela—Valencia. | Marital violence—Venezuela. | Women, Crimes against—Venezuela. | BISAC BIOGRAPHY & AUTOBIOGRAPHY / Sports | SPORTS & RECREATION / Boxing | BIOGRAPHY & AUTOBIOGRAPHY / Cultural, Ethnic & Regional / Hispanic & Latino
Classification: LCC GV1131.S77 2019 | DDC 796.8/3/092—dc23

Hamilcar Publications
An imprint of Hannibal Boxing Media
Ten Post Office Square, 8th Floor South
Boston, MA 02109
www.hamilcarpubs.com

Printed in the United States of America

On the cover: *Champion Edwin Valero punches challenger Hector Velazquez during a fight for the WBA lightweight world title in Caracas, Venezuela, on December 20, 2009.*

Frontispiece: *Jennifer Carolina Viera de Valero watches the fight between Edwin Valero and Antonio DeMarco for the WBC world lightweight title at Arena Monterrey in Monterrey, Mexico, on February 6, 2010.*

To those who thought they were seeing the next big thing

CONTENTS

Birth of a Nightmare

Few things are sadder than the truly monstrous.
—Nathanael West, *The Day of the Locust.*

During the early morning hours of Sunday, April 18, 2010, in the lobby of a hotel in Valencia, Carabobo, one of the best fighters Venezuela had ever produced spoke quietly with his wife. He was a celebrity in his country, a fiercely patriotic man, a proud father of two. Though the couple presented a relaxed picture, the poor woman was probably shaking with worry. Edwin Valero, twenty-eight, had for weeks seemed hell-bent on killing her.

The hotel staff may have sensed that Valero's circuitry wasn't quite right, and hadn't been for a long time. The feelings of paranoia that had jabbed at him in recent times were now wading in with more withering volleys: the suspicion that his wife was having an affair; the fear that people meant to do him harm; and the fear that police, gangsters, even his own mother were conspiring against him.

Ugly stories seeped out of Venezuela. Valero was unhinged and out of control. He'd spent nine days in psychiatric care. His wife had been hospitalized with mysterious injuries. Yet his manager was still trying to set up a fight for him in Mexico. Valero hadn't yet fought a major opponent, but pundits had dubbed him the sport's next moneymaker. He was the fantasy of all boxing fans, a reformed street fighter with a sledgehammer punch who didn't even need proper leverage to knock opponents cold.

"He loved to be in the ring," said Rudy Hernandez, a trainer who knew Valero in earlier days. "I told him, 'The difference between you and a lot of other fighters here is that you love being in the ring. That's why you're going to be a superstar. Keep working as hard as you do, and you'll be the next superstar of boxing.'"

He'd come at opponents like an evil spirit. He was a bizarre vision of a fighter: he'd charge in with his hands low, his eyes ablaze with cold fire. Sometimes he'd yell or hiss when he threw punches. To be in the ring with him must have been nightmarish. "There is something inside me that I have to unleash on someone," Valero once said. "Perhaps it's anger, hatred I feel at having been denied a childhood."

Gales of paranoia whipped through his mind now. Increasingly distrustful and depressed, Valero had spent the weeks after his latest victory arguing with family members and embarrassing himself in public. He believed criminals from Venezuela's underworld were following him. He confessed to a doctor that he was a drug addict. He told his manager that events in his childhood haunted him.

He was in a morbid tailspin. A psychologist said Valero's problems stemmed from an old head injury and extended drug use. The word "psychotropic" appeared repeatedly in medical reports.

Just two months earlier he'd scored an impressive tenth-round stoppage of Antonio DeMarco, a solid fighter who some had predicted would stand up to Valero. In the early rounds, DeMarco boxed well. Yet Valero grew stronger with each passing round, roaring forward like the living bulldozer in Theodore Sturgeon's old science fiction tale, *Killdozer*. DeMarco's corner, realizing their man was done, stopped the fight after the ninth. It was the greatest victory of Valero's career, but after this bout his strange behavior reached a scary crescendo.

The fighter's wife, Jennifer, had dealt with his behavior for years. For reasons known only to other women who endure abusive husbands, she stayed with him. Perhaps it was for the sake of their two children, eight-year-old Edwin Jr., and five-year-old Jennifer Roselyn. Valero loved his children. He had been abandoned by his own father and vowed to give his son and daughter the love he hadn't been given. But bizarre things happened around the Valero home. He once took Jennifer to the hospital with a bullet wound in her left leg. He said gangsters had driven by their home in Caracas and shot her. Meanwhile, he had his chest tattooed with the face of Venezuela's president Hugo Chávez and played around with unregistered guns.

As the clock reached 1:35 a.m., Edwin and Jennifer made their way to room 624. Valero had asked the staff to check under the bed to make sure no one was hiding there. He believed someone had been following him and Jennifer all night. Once he was satisfied the room was empty, he and Jennifer went inside. There's no telling what went on during the next few hours, or where his paranoia took him, but in that room something terrible happened. At 5:30 a.m. Valero appeared in the lobby. As calmly as one might order something from room service, he told the staff that he had just killed his wife.

• • •

He was a storyteller.

He described his early days as if he'd been born in the Seventh Circle of Hell. People absorbed the stories and spewed them out in different ways. Some said he'd been a homeless child, starving in the street. Others said he was an industrious little kid who went door to door selling bags of garlic to housewives. You get the sense that he had some unimaginably hard times but manufactured a frightening autobiography to amuse people. He was selling uplift and desperation.

We know his father left the family. Edwin mentioned it in practically every interview. The father, Antonio Domingo, eventually got sick of being the villain in his son's story.

"Ask my other children if I have been a bad father," he said. "I left the house because of problems with his mother, but I never abandoned them, I was always aware and I helped them financially. Edwin told me one day: 'Dad, I say all that because it gives me more fame, so they see me as the child who suffered a lot.'"

Domingo asked Valero to stop telling those stories. Valero never stopped. Valero controlled the narrative. He was hawking poor pitiful me.

Yet, even if he enjoyed portraying himself as the forsaken child who fought his way out of the rubble of Venezuela, other family members say Valero's childhood was indeed traumatizing for him. He cried often, even as an adult. He was stuck on the idea that he'd been deprived of a regular upbringing. "Edwin had a void that he never explained," said his younger brother Luis. "He never said what he felt."

Listen to his family and friends. You might find yourself believing he never touched drugs until the months before he killed Jennifer. Listen to them. You might even believe he didn't kill her. You might end up believing the stories about kidnappers and thugs and government conspiracies.

The trainers and sparring partners who knew Valero won't buy that he had major mental malfunctions. A psychologist who diagnosed Valero in Venezuela dropped a word: *schizophrenia*. Valero's old gym acquaintances can't accept such things. He'd been too focused. He could hit a heavy bag so hard that the foundation of the city seemed to quake. How could such a good fighter be schizophrenic? Old-time head doctors had a term for it: *funneling*. A person like Valero could focus on something with a sniper's precision even as his mind frayed at the edges. It's that ability to focus that kept the bad thoughts at bay. Of course, this kind of focus only works for a while. The mind falls in on itself.

Jennifer was no match for him. Valero once told a reporter he wished he could keep his wife and children in a crystal box so no harm could come to them. When she was found dead, the blood from her slit throat had clotted on the hotel carpet. It looked like a small pig had been slaughtered. Still, her body was placed on the floor very much like a little doll in a box.

Some reports said he had taken her to the hotel against her will. Others said they were both on the way to a rehab center in Cuba. She was a drug user. She needed help too. The story has two sides. And with each side, there are those who deny and debate and disbelieve.

You could tell it as a straight psycho tale. You could simply focus on her injuries. The bite marks. The gunshot wound. The perforated lung. The time she overdosed and nearly fell off the roof of their apartment. The sad look on her face as she sat ringside. He's winning championships. She's fearing for her life.

You could tell it that way. You could get away with it. There's a thirst for madness. You could draw from a big pool of nasty details and rumors.

He had secrets. We learned enough of them to think we knew him. We'll never know him.

The Venezuelan media treated the Valero case as a tragedy. The American coverage made it a horror story. It's possible that it was both. You take what you need and project it to your audience. Americans like to judge; Venezuelans wanted a hero.

He's dead now. Mental illness and drug addiction took him down. He was found in a jail cell, a picture of his family stuffed into his mouth.

He's dead now.

He doesn't care how the story is told.

• • •

Edwin Antonio Valero Vivas was born in Bolero Alto, a tiny village in Merida, Venezuela, on December 3, 1981. Wedged between three national parks, Bolero Alto, is part of a parish named after Gabriel Picón González, a war hero who helped win the Battle of Los Horcones in 1813. It was a place where superstition still lived, where the elders might tell stories of babies being snatched by river witches. Less than 100 miles away is Lake Maracaibo, where on most nights of the year you can see terrifying

5

lightning storms at the mouth of the Catatumbo River. The indigenous storytellers claimed this odd atmospheric phenomenon, which could produce up to 240 lightning strikes in an hour, was actually millions of fireflies trying to communicate with the earth. The image of these ruthless electrical storms suited Edwin, a restless boy embarking on his own stormy future, a boy born with lightning in his fists.

The third child born to Eloisa and Antonio Domingo Valero, Edwin came into the world as Venezuela was enjoying an unprecedented boxing heyday, with Ernesto España and Antonio Esparragoza earning accolades and championships. Edwin learned that he, too, could fight. Even at a young age he was brawling in the streets, settling arguments by throwing punches.

When Edwin was seven, his father left the family for another woman. For the rest of his life, Edwin would portray his father's departure as an apocalyptic event.

Eloisa moved the brood north to La Palmita. She took a job in El Vigia as a dishwasher. Edwin and his older brother Edward worked selling fruit and spices in El Vigia's Railway Plaza.

A vibrant city located on the Chama River, El Vigia's hallmarks included the magnificent Cathedral of Our Lady of Perpetual Help, plus factories, shopping plazas, universities, parks, and a baseball stadium. Being the second-largest city in Merida, El Vigia must have seemed to Edwin like a futuristic metropolis.

The brothers also worked in a bicycle shop owned by a former fighter, Dimas Garcia. When Edwin said he would like to be a boxer someday, Garcia told him the business was too dangerous.

But Valero had known danger from a young age. Though El Vigia was a sophisticated city, it was a haven for pickpockets, kidnappers, and drug dealers. Like many poor boys from the country, Valero was drawn to the city's dark underbelly. When he wasn't selling fruit, Valero was running with kid gangs. He had become a little criminal. His mother couldn't control him. Edwin was a wild, dirty child, unwilling to bathe or wear shoes.

Yet Eloisa never believed Edwin was as bad as his friends. She alleged that his new pals had even killed people. Edwin, she said, "was not a bad boy. Just a little bit off."

Valero started drinking at age nine and using drugs at eleven. At thirteen he dropped out of school and enrolled in a tae kwon do academy. When his mother claimed the classes were too expensive, he quit and went back to selling garlic. Valero would later describe these years as "work, work, work."

Sometimes he'd add his catchphrase: "I didn't have a normal childhood."

• • •

Francisco "Morochito" Rodríguez was one of the country's most acclaimed amateur fighters. He remains the only Venezuelan boxer to ever win a gold medal at the Olympics, doing so at the 1968 Mexico games. Rodríguez used his fame to establish a small boxing gym in El Vigia. One day on his garlic route, Edwin noticed the place offered free boxing lessons. He convinced Edward that they should look into it.

Oscar Ortega took pity on the boys. Ortega was a respected boxing coach in El Vigia. When he found out Edwin and Edward couldn't afford bus fare home and were sometimes sleeping on the streets, he let them sleep on the gym benches at night. He also made sure they were fed. Years later, Valero would ask Ortega to be his godfather.

"Boxing just attracted me somehow," Valero said, "and I decided to give it a try. One week later, I was living in the gym, where professor Oscar Ortega formed me as a fighter."

Ortega liked this feisty little lefthander whose body seemed loaded with springs. Even at thirteen, Valero punched with unusual power. Ortega gave him keys to the place. Edwin would let himself in at night when he had nowhere else to go. Sleeping on hard benches wasn't ideal, but Edwin had a place to dream and think about the future.

Ortega fretted over Valero. The kid was a bit of a loose cannon. Valero would tell his coach, "Don't worry professor. I have my feet on the ground."

Ortega tried to teach Valero that a boxer's life was difficult. One of the country's best, Vicente Paul Rondon, had recently died in a Caracas slum, destitute and forgotten.

Valero had no use for cautionary tales. In fact, Valero was jailed over a dozen times before he was fifteen. (One police file cited forty arrests throughout his life.) Ortega would always bail him out. Valero bragged that he was given preferential treatment because he was an athlete. Still, he couldn't curb his taste for larceny.

He robbed local university students, stealing small motorbikes and storing them in the gym. He later claimed his bike stealing got him six months in jail, which convinced him to get out of the criminal life. Other sources mention a seven-month stint for assaulting a woman at gunpoint. Valero is also believed to have shot and killed a rival over a stolen motorcycle. He hid out for weeks in Caracas like a fugitive.

Many look back at Valero's young life and say he was simply a rebel who did as he pleased. But Valero's dual personality—diligent athlete by day, street hooligan by night—reflected Venezuela's own double nature.

Venezuela is a country where luxury hotels are side by side with shanty-towns. It's an oil-rich country but has tottered for years on the brink of economic disaster. It was once the wealthiest country in Latin America, yet many homes are without floors or windows. The country is famous for beauty pageants, but its rate of violence against women is among the world's highest. The country is beautiful, known for mountains and lakes and religious statuary—a 153-foot concrete Virgin Mary stands on a hill in Trujillo like a bored sentinel—yet Venezuela is one the most crime-ridden countries in the world. Glossy tourist pamphlets advise visitors to not go out at night.

Venezuela's escalating crime rate was a result of the 1970s oil boom. Encouraged by the swift growth of the cities, a glut of country people drifted into urban areas. The result was overcrowding and a lot of unemployed young men. Boys who had been the sons of farmers became robbers. They formed kidnapping rings. This was Valero's world.

Unlawful activities aside, Valero's life took another turn when he was seventeen. That's when he noticed a pretty girl whose aunt lived near the gym. She was Jennifer Carolina Viera Finol, a thirteen-year-old student at Simon Bolivar High School. She was of Portuguese descent, dark haired, dark eyed, willowy. She was a typical Venezuelan girl, one who imagined she would be a model or a pageant winner. Edwin told his buddies that Jennifer would someday be his wife. Jennifer's sister, Andreína, introduced them.

Edwin and Jennifer grew close quickly. He picked her up at school every afternoon on his yellow Yamaha motorcycle. Jennifer's parents objected. Then they relented. They could see the pair were in love.

By the time Jennifer turned fourteen, Valero had convinced her to be with him forever. It would be years before they were officially married, but they drove off in a banana truck to live together in Tovar, twenty-six miles west of Caracas.

At the time, it probably seemed like the height of romance.

• • •

Young love didn't interrupt Valero's amateur boxing career. He won eighty-six bouts, losing only six. He won three consecutive national amateur championships. He'd found his calling.

He journeyed to Argentina to qualify for the 2000 Olympics. He lost on points to Brazil's Valdemir Pereira. After that, he took the wrong bus home from the Caracas airport. He found himself in an unfamiliar neighborhood. Bandits took his passport, his money, even his silver qualifying medal. He cried for two weeks.

Valero would, however, win the 2000 Central America and Caribbean Championship in Caracas, defeating Francisco Bojado for the gold medal.

Bojado would be Mexico's Olympic representative that year in Australia. Beating him must have given Valero some satisfaction. The fight was close, but Valero stunned Bojado in the final round. He impressed Bojado's trainer, Joe Hernandez. "He was," Hernandez would say years later, "a monster."

As he entered manhood, Valero stood a bit over five feet six, and weighed around 126 pounds. He was the size of Antonio Esparragoza, the power-punching star from Cumaná. Esparragoza had represented Venezuela at the 1980 Moscow Olympics, turned pro the year Valero was born, and enjoyed a four-year reign as WBA featherweight champion. Valero admired Esparragoza but told his coach that he wanted to be even greater, to be world famous like Muhammad Ali. It was a grand vision. Even the best Venezuelan fighters rarely fought outside of Latin America.

Still, it appeared Valero was turning pro at a good time. Though heavyweights had always taken the spotlight, some of the most popular fighters in the business—Johnny Tapia, Marco Antonio Barrera, Erik Morales, and a new star, Manny Pacquiao—were in the featherweight range. They fought in Las Vegas and were featured on HBO. Valero and his team must have been encouraged by the growing prestige of the lighter fighters. With a style suited to the professional ranks, and a hunger for fame, Valero could invade these lower weight classes like the Visigoths sacking Rome. Perhaps, unlike most Venezuelan fighters, he'd leave his mark in America.

But the story nearly ended before it began.

On February 5, 2001, Valero was ripping down the street on a motorcycle. His father had been in a car accident, and he was on his way to help him. Stories varied. Either Valero slammed into a car and hit his head on the back windshield, or he flew over the car and landed headfirst on some asphalt. He wasn't wearing a helmet.

He spent thirteen days in a hospital. Doctors found a small blood clot between Valero's scalp and skull—not in his brain. They gave him a choice: he could wait six months to see if the clot would clear up on its own, or they could operate and remove it. Wanting to get out of the hospital and resume his boxing career, he opted for a relatively simple procedure where the clot was drained. It wasn't considered major surgery. He probably thought that was the end of the matter. He was nineteen years old, strong as an ox, and crafty as a rat. He had Jennifer at his side and a promising future as a boxer. A little knock on the head wouldn't stop him.

• • •

Seventeen months later, on July 9, 2002, Valero made his professional boxing debut at United Nations Park in Caracas. He needed just a bit over two minutes to knock out a fellow named Eduardo Hernandez.

Hernandez never fought again.

The months after Valero's surgery had been torturous. He wasn't allowed to fight right away. He took odd jobs to support himself and Jennifer but proved inept at everything. In March, Edwin Jr. was born, adding to Valero's pressures. Broke and desperate, Valero enlisted in the Venezuelan army. After two busts for fighting, he was dishonorably discharged.

"I like to hit men," Valero said years later. "It liberates me."

Valero finished out 2002 with first-round knockouts over Danny Sandoval, Alirio Rivero, Luis Soto, and Julio Pineda.

Pineda never fought again.

Sandoval tried Valero a second time in March 2003, but again, it was lights out in one round. In May, Edgar Mendoza fell to Valero in the first.

Mendoza never fought again.

The Valero of these early fights was calm, efficient. He had a picturesque right jab. He looked like an archer when he threw it. He threw his left cross with supreme confidence. His trainer at the time was Jorge Zerpa, an experienced hand.

In May 2003, Valero was matched against Colombian Dairo Julio. Though decidedly better than Valero's previous victims, Julio failed to get out of the first round.

11

Valero was 8-0, with eight knockouts. A Valero representative contacted Joe Hernandez in California to assist with Valero's American debut.
Remembering Valero from the 2000 Caracas tournament, Hernandez was
eager to see how the kid had improved. He would soon hail Valero as the
best prospect to come out of Venezuela in thirty years.

• • •

From the moment Valero entered the Maywood Boxing Gym in Los Angeles,
Hernandez saw immediately that someone new and unusual had arrived.

He had high cheekbones and piercing eyes. He looked regal, carrying himself like he'd already been a champion for years. The only thing
that ruined the picture was an explosion of acne that covered much of
his face, as if teen hormones still percolated inside him. Valero was fighting at super-featherweight, but his frame could easily carry another ten
or fifteen pounds. He was raw, high spirited, with extraordinary power
and speed. Hernandez tended to time rounds at four and a half minutes,
and Valero would punch nonstop. Sometimes he seemed unpolished.
Sometimes he looked like a veteran who knew every move in the book.

Hernandez noticed the effect Valero had on sparring partners: No one
could last two rounds with him. Hernandez paid fighters extra to work
with Valero, but they wouldn't do it. Mike Anchondo, a future titleholder
and a Maywood gym regular, asked Hernandez, "What do you feed this
guy? Nails?"

It was decided to bring in Juan Lazcano, "The Hispanic Causing
Panic." Lazcano was bigger than Valero and a veteran of nearly forty
fights. Preparing for a bout in Las Vegas and on the brink of major recognition, Lazcano agreed to spar with the young Venezuelan. Lazcano,
who had defeated some quality fighters, must have hated the experience.
Though stories differ as to how many rounds he actually sparred with
Valero, the one thing all agree on is that Lazcano never came back. He left
his gloves and other boxing gear behind, never to claim them.

There were times in Maywood when Valero seemed to defy logic. Many southpaws look awkward in the ring, but Valero was fluid, graceful, athletic. There was such precision in his work that he seemed less like a boxer and more like a fencing master. He was cocky, too. He would tell Hernandez that he was going to hurt his sparring partner with a particular punch, and then he'd do it. Hernandez would tell him to take it easy on his poor sparring partners, but Valero was impulsive. Hernandez once compared Valero to Michael Jordan. "It was that kind of ability," the trainer said.

Urbano Antillon was a sturdy Mexican-American super-featherweight from Maywood. He sparred a few times with Valero, but he wasn't impressed. The next time they sparred, Valero hit him so hard that Antillon's head swiveled and his legs shuddered. The session was stopped.

Brian Harty was on hand to record some of Valero's workouts for Maxboxing.com. He recalls Valero as tireless, almost robotic. Valero might have cracked a joke in between workouts, but once he was focused, his concentration was unbreakable. "It's impossible to know if the way I describe him now is affected by what ultimately happened," Harty said, "but there was just a constant buzz around him—and I mean like an electric buzz, like one of those bug zappers. I can't imagine him sleeping."

Valero buzzed his way through a number of LA gyms, from the fancy ones with modern equipment to the ones where salsa music blared from the house speakers and old fight posters seemed stuck to the walls through sheer humidity. He was like a gunslinger walking into a new town. Nobody knew who he was. There were only whispers and rumors about this gym gypsy who knocked people around. He'd smash them on the arms, in the ribs. Sometimes he'd hit a guy a few times and the guy would simply quit. If someone stayed with him for a few rounds, Valero would playfully pat him on the shoulder at the end of the session.

"He obviously enjoyed being in the gym," Harty said. "I don't know how a person is able to summon punch after punch with such aggression like he did, though. Whatever was driving him, it was always right there below the surface for him to tap into."

13

Hernandez invited members of the local media to watch Valero spar. Among the first to see him was Doug Fischer of Maxboxing.com. In a 2004 column for ESPN.com, Fischer described what had seemed like a once-in-a-lifetime thrill.

"Only two fighters that I have witnessed train in the past ten years come close to Valero's athletic perfection, Shane Mosley and Floyd Mayweather Jr.—and I'm talking about these two multi-champs when they were at their physical peaks," Fischer wrote. "Valero's aggression, bursting speed, brute strength, and intensity reminded me of the lightweight version of Mosley. His poise, technique, balance, and craftiness reminded me of the '97–'99 version of Mayweather."

Though Valero and Jennifer had an apartment, he spent much of his time in tiny quarters he shared with Hernandez, Anchondo, and Daniel Ponce de Leon, a strong Mexican southpaw who would soon become quite successful. Fischer recalled the volatile natures of Valero and his stablemates, especially with the addition of alcohol. There had been a particularly nasty brawl between Valero and de Leon in a Dallas hotel lobby. "There were chairs turned over and blood everywhere," Fischer said. "These three, they had a particular dysfunction with alcohol. When they got drunk, they got crazy." Valero was already stubborn with a temper. When alcohol was introduced, Fischer reckoned, Valero became "a maniac."

In de Leon, Valero met his equal. De Leon was known to rip off his shirt in a bar and challenge a rival to fight bare-knuckle. "The story I heard was that de Leon bit off a piece of Valero's ear," Fischer said. "That's why Valero started growing his hair out."

Valero's main beef with Anchondo and de Leon was rooted in envy. They had main-event status on local shows, and received monthly stipends. In Valero's eyes, Anchondo and de Leon were inferior. The truth was that Valero wasn't well connected. Anchondo had been a pro for three years, and de Leon had been on the Mexican Olympic team in 2000. Valero, conversely, had been fighting in Venezuelan backwaters. "He was a gamble," said Fischer. Joe Hernandez was acting as Valero's manager

14

and trainer. Oscar De La Hoya's father Joel was a silent partner. There wasn't much careful planning involved with Valero. "It was more like, 'Let's take a gamble on this guy.'"

Sometimes Valero's wrath was directed at Hernandez. "They split every month," said Fischer. "Little things would set Valero off. For instance, Joe was very old school, and when the guys appeared in public at a boxing event, Joe wanted them to dress up. Valero thought he was being disrespected. He'd say, 'Fuck it. I'll train myself.' But Valero liked Joe, and he'd come back."

"He wasn't a sweet kid," said Hernandez.

Despite the drinking and flare-ups, Valero was generally likable. "He was quiet," said Fischer. "Respectful. Shy. He kept to himself. When he trained, it was like no one else existed. He was in his own little world. But if he talked to you he'd be really cool and sincere. He took pride in himself. And when he shook your hand, he *crushed* it."

Valero occasionally talked to his new associates about his criminal past. He said he had known thirty people who were already dead and buried. In El Vigia, Valero said, one had to be either a drug dealer or an assassin. He claimed a contract had been taken out on him, but the killer who drew the assignment was a friend and couldn't do it. Why the contract wasn't given to someone else was a detail Valero didn't explain.

The impression Valero gave was that boxing had saved his life. Without boxing, he said repeatedly, he'd be in prison or dead.

• • •

Valero's first professional bout in America took place on July 19, 2003, at the Activities Center of Maywood—which has since become Maywood's YMCA—on the undercard of a show headlined by de Leon. Valero was matched with Emmanuel Ford, a thirty-two-year-old with a record of 5-20-2. Ford was on the canvas three times before the bout was stopped in the first.

Five weeks later, Valero fought at the Marriot Hotel in Irvine, California. On a card headlined by female minimumweights, Valero met Roque Cassiani, a thirty-three-year-old Colombian who had been in the ring with some good fighters. Valero knocked him out in the first. After a return to Caracas to score a one-round knockout of Alejandro Heredia, it was back to Irvine. This time Valero faced a 0-4 opponent named Tomas Zambrano. As had become his signature, Valero needed less than a round to win.

Valero was 12-0 with twelve knockouts. None of his opponents had heard the bell for the second round. He'd already fought three times in America, more than most Venezuelan fighters. He'd even signed a contract with Oscar De La Hoya's Golden Boy Promotions, only in its second year of operation but considered a major promotional firm. The plan was to bring Valero to New York for an HBO fight against Francisco Lorenzo, a respectable fighter from the Dominican Republic.

The excitement came to an abrupt end in January 2004. The reason: Valero failed his prefight physical. The examination by the New York State Athletic Commission revealed a tiny blemish on Valero's brain. The commission's medical policy in such cases was to recommend the denial of a boxing license in New York and an indefinite medical suspension.

Valero explained about the motorcycle accident, but Dr. Barry D. Jordan, NYSAC's chief medical officer, was unbending. If an injury from years earlier could still be traced on an MRI, Valero was undoubtedly at risk. The doctor advised him to retire. The Association of Boxing Commissions backed the NYSAC decision.

Within a few weeks, Valero went from being Golden Boy Promotions' hot new fighter to being banned in the United States.

• • •

On May 21, 2005, Valero was in Caseros, Buenos Aires, receiving a warm welcome from a small but rowdy boxing crowd. His opponent, Hernan Abraham Valenzuela, was beaten down at 2:10 of the first.

Seventeen months had passed since Valero's last bout, an eternity for a young fighter trying to establish himself. In that time he'd undergone examinations by several neurosurgeons and was judged fit to fight. Golden Boy Promotions attempted to overturn the New York ruling, but failed. Valero said he was willing to fight in other countries, but he was warned that such a move might result in his being barred from the States forever.

In April 2005, Valero was dropped from the Golden Boy roster.

After living in Los Angeles for several months, and working for a spell as a cab driver to make ends meet, Valero returned to Venezuela. He and Jennifer now had a second child, Jennifer Roselyn, born in LA.

Valero was frustrated. He took the first opportunity that was offered. He passed his prefight physical and readied to fight in Argentina.

There were rumors of a mysterious fax sent to the WBA by Golden Boy, warning them of Valero's suspension and suggesting he was a risk. The promotional group denied sending it, but Valero was already tired of De La Hoya's fledgling company. He didn't understand how they couldn't fix a medical issue in New York. "If you ask any trainer or fighter," Valero sneered, "they wouldn't say a good thing about that company."

Having been cleared by medical experts around the world—including the surgeon who had once operated on Elizabeth Taylor's brain tumor—Valero claimed he was being held back for political reasons. He pointed out that Marco Antonio Barrera, another Golden Boy fighter, had undergone a serious brain operation years earlier and was fighting all the time. Valero felt Barrera received special treatment by Golden Boy. He fumed.

The bout in Buenos Aires, though, appeared to hearten Valero. He'd remember it as a special night.

The finish was electric. He dropped Valenzuela once, and then went left-hand crazy to finish him off. A white towel came flying in from Valenzuela's corner to signify surrender. As referee Guillermo Pineda moved in to stop the bout, Valero landed two more punches, haymakers reaching back to the alleys of El Vigia. Valenzuela sagged along the ropes, out on his feet.

Valero jogged around inside the ring, howling and sticking his tongue out at the crowd.

Ironically, the bout was part of a WBA-sponsored event with an "anti-drug" message. It was called "KO Drugs."

• • •

Less than two months after his bout in Argentina, Valero was in Panama City fighting in an arena named after Roberto Duran, against an opponent seemingly named after one of Duran's great rivals, Esteban de Jesús Morales. Valero stopped Morales in one round.

There were murmurs that Valero had set some sort of record by beginning his career with fourteen consecutive first-round knockouts.

"I'm happy to hear that I hold a world record," Valero said. "That means I'd have already achieved something big if I'd retire today."

Valero was entering his wilderness years. Though several important promoters expressed interest in him, no contracts were forthcoming. He put up an optimistic front, but later said the New York ban had left him devastated. In 2006, when his fortunes changed for the better, Valero recalled this tough year. "Things happen for a reason," he said. "I did not let myself be defeated. I did suffer. I cried, I was depressed, I went through a little bit of everything."

Valero made the best of the situation by taking a trio of "stay busy" bouts, one in Venezuela, one in Japan, and one in France. The opposition was weak, and the paydays were minimal.

Historians dug up Arthur Susskind, a Jewish lightweight from a century earlier. Fighting as "Young Otto," Susskind started his career with sixteen first-round stoppages, a record no one had ever recognized or cared about. Valero broke Otto's record in Paris when he crushed Aram Ramazyan twenty seconds into the first. From then on Valero would be introduced as being in the Guinness Book of World Records.

Knockout streaks were entertaining, but when Joe Hernandez saw tapes of Valero in this period, he claimed Valero looked worse than when he first arrived in Maywood.

"He was trying to knock people out without even thinking," said Hernandez.

Perhaps it was the adrenaline of being in the ring for money, or perhaps he was becoming too concerned about scoring first-round knockouts. Whatever the reason, Valero no longer concerned himself with finesse.

In Japan, for instance, against a chap named Hero Bando, Valero looked awful, swinging away like an excitable rookie. Of course, once Valero connected, Bando fell so hard he bounced.

The promoter, Akohiko Honda, had promised Bando a bonus if he survived the first round. The bout was going to be televised in Japan, so Honda wanted a few rounds of action. When Valero heard Bando was offered roughly a thousand dollars if he went beyond three minutes, he suggested he should get the bonus if he beat Bando in one round. The promoter was amused by Valero and agreed.

The Bando bout was Valero's first under the auspices of Japan's Teiken Promotions. Honda, Teiken's chief, was an important figure in Japanese boxing. Honda had clout—and had eyes for Valero.

"For Valero to respect you," said Fischer, "you had to have been around. Young guys were always approaching him with offers to train or manage him, and he'd say, 'Who the fuck are you? What do you know?' He wanted experienced people. Valero saw how people listened to Honda. He realized this was a guy who could help him."

Valero signed a contract to fight in Japan. If America didn't want him, he'd be a road warrior.

• • •

Valero began 2006 with another bout in Venezuela. On February 25, at a recreation center in Turmero, Valero knocked out Whyber Garcia at

2:57 of the first round. The win earned Valero something called the WBA super-featherweight *Fedelatin* title, a belt rarely mentioned outside of Latin American countries.

Exactly one month later, Valero fought Genaro Trazancos in Hyogo, Japan. For the first time, Valero was forced to go into the second round of a contest, which only meant Trazancos took a lopsided beating into 1:38 of round two.

Japan had an effect on Valero. He was making more money than ever. He had lackeys and yes-men. He was getting star treatment.

"Valero's whole style changed when he started fighting in Japan," said Harty. "From what I heard it was partially because he was being paid a bonus if he could knock the guy out in the first round. It had become sort of a gimmick with him, so he was just going in there and swinging like a caveman." The changes in Valero were not restricted to his work in the ring. "I remember being shocked the first time I saw him at a press event during that time, because it was like he'd had a makeover. He was wearing fashionable clothes, had some small trendy glasses on, he'd grown out his hair; I think that might've been when he started doing the goatee."

When Valero was asked about Japan, he said only that he could find better sparring partners there than in Venezuela. "I am very dedicated to my work," he said. "I do not really have any friends. Any trainer in Venezuela, even if they do not like my personality, cannot say anything negative about my training habits. Mr. Honda, being a businessman, I think, was attracted to me because of my work ethic."

It was also around this time that Valero dumped his nickname—"El Inca." He'd never liked it. A company called "El Inca" had sponsored him early in his career, so he'd worn the name on his trunks for a few fights. He'd wanted to be known as "El Coli," or "The Hummingbird," a nickname he sometimes used for Jennifer.

For years Valero had been known as "El Inca." The name fit. It was a tribute to the indigenous people of South America. It had panache. It conjured up ancient empires and lost cities of gold. In the coming years he would be "El Dinamita," then "El Liquidator" and "El Terminator." In Japan he was known as "Kaminari," or "The Lightning Man." None of those names stuck. In Venezuela, he was always "El Inca." Even Valero's family members referred to him as "El Inca."

Somehow, beating a string of unknowns earned Valero a title shot. On August 5, 2006, he would be in Panama City to face WBA super-featherweight titlist Vicente Mosquera. Regardless of how the fight was made—WBA headquarters was in Venezuela, and the organization had always been cozy with Venezuelan fighters—Mosquera was a significant step up in competition for Valero. Known as "El Loco," Mosquera was a strong boxer who had won twenty-four of twenty-six bouts. He was also Panamanian, and had done most of his fighting in Panama. Valero was going to Mosquera's turf.

Then again, a coyote might wander onto your property to eat your dog.

• • •

For the first time in his pro career, Valero found a suitable rival in Mosquera. You don't get a name like "El Loco" by being delicate.

Mosquera didn't fear Valero. He even bested Valero in some prefight trash talk. At a press event, as the exchange of words was heating up, Valero noticed the greatest Panamanian fighter of all, Roberto Duran, in the crowd. Impulsively, Valero stepped down from the stage to have his picture taken with Duran. Then, reluctantly, he returned to the podium.

Valero went through the motions, but press events bored him. "I go to the press conference because it is my duty as a boxer," he'd later say. "I just want to train well, make my money, and fight."

Things got worse during the weigh-in. Panamanian fans yelled "Payaso"—Spanish for "clown"—as Valero stepped onto the scale. He'd learned that a local casino had installed Mosquera as a 3-1 favorite to retain the championship. Mosquera stalked around with his shirt off.

21

He looked lean and ready. He barked insults at Valero. It was basic stuff. "You're not a man. . . . I'll show you what a man is. . . . Why don't you answer me—are you scared?"

Fight night.

Valero looked tight during the introductions. His face was emotionless, drawn. From the opening bell, Valero seemed stiff. Mosquera startled him with a quick right to the mouth. The punch had the effect of an electric shock. Valero countered, dropping Mosquera to one knee. The Panamanian bounced up before referee Luis Pabon could start a count. Angered at being down in front of his home supporters, Mosquera scored with another right hand to the *boca*. Valero's entire body quivered. It was probably the hardest he'd ever been hit in his career. All of this after less than a minute.

The rest of the round played out at dizzying speed, with Valero throwing his right-left combos, and Mosquera moving in, trying to land his own punches. At one point Mosquera smashed Valero in the face with four consecutive right uppercuts. Valero took them and punched back, wildly. He put Mosquera on the canvas a second time. "El Loco" rose and glowered. The round ended with Mosquera rumbling forward as Valero fired away.

After an equally frenetic second round, with fans chanting "Loco! Loco!" the third saw a couple of firsts for Valero. One, he was in the third round, which he'd not seen since his amateur days. And two, Mosquera knocked him down. The Panama crowd exploded. Valero got up and blinked a few times as Pabon gave him the mandatory eight count.

Valero had found himself in the middle of an epic.

The fighters remained upright during the next few rounds, but the action was no less blistering. Mosquera snapped Valero's head back more than once, causing the Panamanians to roar. Valero fired back. It was a battle of wills. Valero's early stiffness had melted away. Now his punches flowed in the classic manner, though sometimes he looked like he was attacking Mosquera with a hatchet.

In the fifth, Mosquera stunned Valero with a low blow. Valero went to his knees and took a timeout. He recuperated. By the eighth it was Mosquera who looked tired.

Valero had never gone past the second round in his pro career, yet he stormed out for the ninth and rained all kinds of hell on Mosquera. Valero knew that something had to give. He'd either break Mosquera's skull, or he'd break his hands trying. Mosquera was weakening. He had the look of an angry drunk. His face was swollen. His left cheek was sliced open. He seemed ready to fall. In the middle of the tenth round, as Valero punched Mosquera around the ring, a thoughtful member of Mosquera's corner stepped through the ropes to stop the fight. Pabon motioned him back and then stopped it himself. Mosquera didn't protest. He'd be taken to a nearby clinic with a dislocated shoulder.

And so it was, at 2:00 of the tenth round in Panama City, on an August evening in 2006, at the Figali Convention Center, Edwin Valero was awarded the WBA super-featherweight title belt. He whooped a couple of times, but considering the long, twisting path he'd taken to get to this point, he was subdued. Valero later explained his low-key behavior. He said that he was looking for Jennifer and couldn't find her. Instead, strangers surrounded him. "I could not enjoy that moment as I would have liked," he said.

The coronation may have been anticlimactic, but no matter what else happened in his crazy life, Edwin Valero would always be called "champion."

• • •

Valero was leery of the fame he'd once craved. In one of the first interviews he gave after beating Mosquera, he sounded unsure about his future. He worried about bringing his family to so many different countries.

By the same token, he knew Venezuela was dangerous. And living in Venezuela would become even more dangerous if he became successful.

23

Celebrities were targets. If he became too famous and his face started appearing on billboards, he'd be putting his family at risk. The idea sickened him.

"I'm afraid of fame," Valero said. "To me it is enough just to be able to fulfill some whims, like having a good car, and good clothes."

He knew Los Angeles was a better location for a fighter, and still harbored hopes that he'd fight in the States.

But one new development in Venezuela intrigued him: he'd received a congratulatory phone call from president Hugo Chávez. He'd been wearing Chávez's image on his trunks for a while, and though Valero didn't want to mix politics and sports, he considered Chávez the greatest thing to happen to Venezuela. Chávez was helping the poor, and Valero claimed Chávez had even helped his mother and some of his relatives when they had serious health problems. "It was very exciting when I spoke with him on the phone," said Valero. "He told me he was proud of me and wanted to see me."

Starstruck, the boxer continued: "The truth is that I was a little nervous. When I return to Venezuela, he will receive me and it will be a real pleasure."

Fame was scary, but Valero liked knowing people in high places.

And Chávez knew exactly how to deal with Valero. When Chávez was introduced to Valero's mother, he jokingly asked to marry her. This way, the president said, he could be Valero's new father.

• • •

By now Valero had a devoted following. Boxing websites covered his fights. The fights could also be seen on the then-fledgling video-sharing site YouTube. Boxing enthusiasts were recording them on DVDs. In Venezuela, where he'd been anonymous, he was finally being mentioned in *El Nacional* and other major newspapers. The attention was coming in big dollops.

Valero was an unexpected gift for fight fans. He wasn't some coddled Olympic medalist. He didn't have the influence of a high-powered promoter behind him. He was a mystery man. He became a popular topic in online forums and on message boards. Stories about his time in Los Angeles spread like folklore, and the legend grew. Like anything else banned in the States—a book, a movie, an automatic weapon—Valero developed a kind of cachet.

It was all about his demeanor: Valero looked the part. Other fighters of the period earned impressive paydays and won fights, but they didn't satisfy anyone's tough-guy fantasies.

De La Hoya? He was cheekily handsome and put out a CD of Spanish ballads. Pacquiao wanted to be a singer, too. Or an actor or politician. Roy Jones Jr. recorded hip-hop tracks and turned out to have a glass jaw. Bernard Hopkins, the great strategist, could be tedious. Shane Mosley smiled too much. Drab Europeans increasingly dominated the heavyweight division. Floyd Mayweather flashed his jewelry but never seemed especially dangerous to anyone's health. Kelly Pavlik looked like the guy coming to clean the furnace.

What boxing fans craved was an outlaw. They wanted a fighter who looked like he could handle himself in the streets. There had been such fighters in the past, fighters who could break your spirit with nothing more than a snarl. This was the secret to Mike Tyson's popularity. But Mike Tyson hadn't been taken seriously in a long time.

Valero had this dangerous quality There was a clip of him at a press conference, speaking at a podium. Jorge Barrios, a South American lightweight known as "The Hyena" started heckling him. They exchanged a few words in Spanish. Valero had said there were too many old duffers in the sport. The new generation would wipe them out. Barrios, a battle-tested veteran, said something like, "Why don't you try it with me?" In a classic street bluff, Valero stepped forward and made Barrios flinch. With Barrios shut down, Valero returned to the podium, unfazed. This was the key to Valero's image: The ring might not be enough for him. He looked like he might drag you into an alley and work you over.

"I like the fist," Valero once said, giving his admirers a perfect quote. "I like to break the face of the man in front of me."

Boxing fans didn't want smiling millionaires with recording contracts. They wanted a destroyer. The wanted someone vicious and unapologetic. Valero fit the role. He was motorcycle crashes and quick knockouts. He was unkempt and untamed.

Valero wasn't without critics, however. Many doubted the worth of his opponents. But for every doubter, there were a growing number of Valero maniacs. And there was no middle ground. You either got on the bandwagon, or you didn't.

Of course, Valero was not as unrefined as his detractors claimed, nor was he as fantastic as his supporters believed. He was somewhere in between.

Valero possessed a couple of traits that marked him as exceptional. The first was his hunter's instinct. He looked at opponents as if they were nothing but potential victims. A lot of fighters have a bit of this, but Valero had it in buckets.

Another rare quality was his ability to punch while moving backward. Most fighters flick a jab when in retreat, but Valero could move back and throw power shots. He was dangerous whether moving forward or backward. Strangest of all was that he could hit with force without having his feet planted. Perfect form wasn't required.

The reason his critics were never on the same page as his backers was due to the distinct difference between the Valero of the gym and the Valero who performed for a paying audience. If in the confines of a gym he was an artist working in miniature, in the arena he worked with bigger, sloppier strokes, creating gaudy murals that could be appreciated from even the cheapest seats. When money was on the line, he wasn't fighting for the connoisseurs; he was fighting for the Philistines. This would be true for the rest of his career. It was just another instance where there seemed to be two Edwin Valeros.

Mad Love

*Domestic abuse starts slowly. If the asshole is on drugs,
it escalates quickly.*
—Nancy Van Tine, Esq.

Weeks after beating Mosquera, Valero's name was mentioned by promoter Bob Arum as a possible opponent for Manny Pacquiao. It could happen in the Philippines, Arum said. The implication was that Valero was just a tune-up for Pacquiao, but just having his name mentioned with Pacquiao's was a welcome change from a year earlier, when Valero was dropped from the Golden Boy roster.

But even as his star was rising, there seemed to be a difference in Valero. It had to do with the way he acted with his family.

In interviews, Valero often praised his wife and children, describing them as "his motor." According to Doug Fischer, Valero had appeared to be a "very loving" husband and father. But there was a noticeable change in Valero after he beat Mosquera. He was still a friendly character on his own, but not around his family. There appeared to be, Fischer noticed, a lack of warmth.

"From that point on," Fischer said, "I never saw them smile. They seemed very solemn. . . . No smiles. Not from the son. Not from the wife." Even Valero's mother, Fischer said, seemed stressed around him.

Jennifer's family recalled a recurring issue about her returning to school to finish her studies. Edwin hated the idea.

"He was jealous," recalled Jennifer's aunt Esmeralda. Valero simply didn't want the young mother of his children "out there." He "took care of her," said Esmeralda, "but never let her go out alone."

Even back in the Los Angeles days, Valero kept Jennifer a bit of a secret.

"I heard from Joe Hernandez that Valero had this beautiful wife, and that he treated her like a prisoner," said Fischer. "Joe didn't say much else, just that Valero was very possessive and controlling. He kept her under lock and key."

• • •

January 3, 2007: Valero is in Tokyo at the Ariake Coliseum, a venue shaped like a flying saucer with seating for 10,000. The new year is barely awake, but he's defending his title against Michael Lozada. Valero knocks him down twice. Lozada tries to continue but his equilibrium is off. He looks like he's just stepped off a carnival ride. Referee Rafael Ramos stops the bout at 1:12 of the first.

"Honda had asked Valero to carry Lozada for a few rounds," recalled Fischer. "I ran into Valero in the lobby on the day of the fight. I said, 'Are you going to carry him?' Valero said, 'No. I feel too good.' That's how he was."

May 3, 2007: Same city. Same location. Valero is defending against the esteemed Japanese titlist, Nobuhito Honmo. Valero uses his right jab more than usual. He's working in a different key. He's methodical. By the eighth, Honmo's face is a mess, like he's been attacked with gardening shears. The ringside doctor suggests the fight be stopped.

Honmo never fights again.

After the bout, Valero is seen holding a small doll. It belongs to Edwin Jr. It's a likeness of his country's president, Hugo Chávez. It is the best-selling Chavecito (Little Chávez) toy.

December 15, 2007: At the Plaza de Toros in Cancun, Mexico, Valero takes on Zaid Zavaleta, a young Mexican fighter known as "The Exterminator." Zavaleta survives a first-round knockdown. He tries some roughhousing in the second; nothing works. Third round: Valero clubs Zavaleta with a right to the jaw. Zavaleta sags. Referee Pabon stops the action at 1:18 of round three. Valero howls. He spits his mouthpiece out and dropkicks it into the audience, sending someone home with a wet souvenir.

It was a nice way to end the year. Three fights. Three wins. Easy money. He was at the top of his game.

• • •

Valero worked hard to sell himself in Japan. He held open workouts at the Teiken Gym in Tokyo. He told a Japanese reporter that he wanted to be "an adopted son of the Japanese people." But even as he praised Japan, he dropped hints that he wasn't opposed to fighting in America. After all, America was where the money was. He also wanted American fans to see his booming punch.

"I know the crowd loves knockouts," Valero said. "It's like hitting a home run or getting a goal in a soccer game."

In between fights, Valero had helped Marco Antonio Barrera prepare for his second bout with Pacquiao, serving as Barrera's sparring partner and playing the role of southpaw. He'd once done the same for Erik Morales.

"Working with these guys is a wonderful assessment tool for me," Valero said. "It lets me know how I match up against the best in the world. At the same time, I get the opportunity to see how they prepare and compare it to my training regimen."

Unfortunately for Valero, that same year saw him involved in a parking-lot skirmish near the Racing Bar, a popular nightclub near Caracas. Reports circulated that Venezuela's young champion had been disfigured.

He spoke to the press immediately.

"First of all," Valero said, "I was attacked. I had not been in a nightclub for seven years and one evening, on an impulse, I decided to go with my wife. So we left our children with my brother and went to the club. I went as far as changing my look and disguising myself when I went to the club, so as not to draw attention. When the night was over and the club was letting out, someone snatched my cell phone. I guess they liked it, since I had brought it to Venezuela from Japan. Anyway, I guess I was then hit with a bottle or a glass, I do not know. Security intervened and that is it. These papers say I was disfigured, which is not true. I did get a cut on my forehead, but it is nothing major."

Valero's supporters were concerned. Was he in the vicinity of his old gang members? Perhaps it was dangerous for him to be back in Venezuela.

Around that time, many near Valero noticed an increase in his temper. He was surly. He blamed it on training. He hated having to lose weight and go without his favorite foods. During the days before a fight he couldn't eat anything except chewing gum.

He'd even broken from his longtime trainer, Jorge Zerpa. The argument had been over the best way to wrap Valero's hands, but Zerpa had noticed Valero was changing. Valero had always been serious in the gym. Now, he'd suddenly interrupt a session to call Hugo Chávez. Sometimes the fighter and the president would talk on the phone for an hour, keeping Zerpa and the sparring partners waiting.

Valero was also drinking more than ever. He'd developed his own favorite concoction—a mouthful of Viagra washed down with tequila. He'd also go days without bathing, out of concern that his body might retain bathwater and make him seem heavier on the scales.

The eccentricities were piling up.

• • •

In the early summer of 2008, Valero was fighting at the Tokyo Budokan, the revered 14,471-seat venue that has hosted everyone from The Beatles to

Led Zeppelin to Muhammad Ali. Valero's challenger, Takehiro Shimada, was an experienced thirty-six-year-old, but after being drilled by a few of Valero's lefts, he decided to survive each round by clinching, or moving around the ring.

At one point in the seventh, after being hit with several hard punches, Shimada went to the ropes and assumed a kneeling position. When the referee hesitated, Valero threw a right to Shimada's head, sending the Japanese challenger into a full sprawl. It was ungentlemanly, hitting a man who seemed to be surrendering, but legal. Duran or Tyson would have done the same. Shimada beat the ten-count, but he looked utterly defeated. The fight was over. It was the first time Shimada had ever been stopped.

Though Valero relied too much on his vaunted left cross, he fought a measured, calculating fight against Shimada. By now he was working with trainer Kenny Adams, an experienced boxing man who had served as head coach for the 1988 American Olympic team. Adams would recall Valero as "a jewel to work with," adding, "we had to get 150-pounders for him to work with, because he was brutal."

Adams did, however, experience Valero's unruly side.

"He drank a little bit, which was kind of a problem," Adams said. "He was *viva loco*, or something like that. In Mexico once, he grabbed me and started choking me. I said, 'You'd better let me go, or I'm gonna bust you.' He said, 'OK Kenny, my friend, my friend.' He was like that. I don't know what it was. He definitely had that streak in him."

St. Louis cruiserweight Ryan Coyne was in several of Valero's training camps during the Adams era. He remembers Valero as both bizarre and awe-inspiring, an athlete who cared nothing about nutrition and "gave zero fucks about what he put into his body," a fighter who eschewed regular training routines yet could always outperform everyone else in the gym.

"Edwin was otherworldly," Coyne said. "He was a world champion drinker. When he sparred, you could smell it on him; the alcohol oozed from his pores. And Edwin never drank water. We'd run six miles, and he'd have four scalding-hot black coffees."

Valero spoke only a bit of English, but he could express himself with facial gestures and body language. "I liked being around him," said Coyne. "He was friendly. Charismatic. He didn't like taking orders, but he wasn't a mean guy. I've never known a more intense person. I remember him pounding on a table, saying that George Bush had sent helicopters to kill Chávez. When he pounded on a table, he got your attention. He could punch through walls.

"I thought there was something unreal about Edwin. The way he'd drink all night, and then come in and train; it's like he was possessed by a devil. I don't want to sound like I'm demonizing him, because I don't mean it that way. I'm not religious, really. I know how weird this sounds, but sometimes I'd watch him and think humans couldn't be that way. There was something supernatural."

Valero was especially unusual in the way he ran. "He was a hard runner," Coyne said. "Even if he'd been drinking all night, he'd just run everybody's dicks into the ground. I could never catch him. I asked him, 'How do you run like that?' Edwin said, 'When you run, you have to run like the police are chasing you, and if they get you, you'll never get out of jail, and you'll never breathe fresh air again.' I'll never forget when he said that. It stayed with me, to this day."

Despite another easy win in Japan, Valero's critics were getting louder. The faultfinders debated whether he should have been disqualified for hitting Shimada while he was kneeling. All agreed that the lineup of limp challengers was getting stale.

Valero's supporters, however, wouldn't bow to the finicky voices on the internet. After all, they'd waited a long time for a fighter like Valero.

He still couldn't fight in the United States. But that was about to change.

● ● ●

The break came unexpectedly.

A court ruling in New York had recently gone in the favor of a fighter who had challenged an "indefinite" medical suspension. The ruling

Edwin and Jennifer got married at the Catholic cathedral in El Vigia on January 5, 2008. For Jennifer it was her long-awaited dream wedding.
Archivo Latino

Edwin and Jennifer with their children Edwin Jr. and
Jennifer Roselyn. In public, the Valeros appeared to
be the perfect family.

Valero with Oscar De La Hoya during
happier times. Eventually their relationship
turned bitter and Valero signed with
De La Hoya's rival promoter, Bob Arum
of Top Rank.

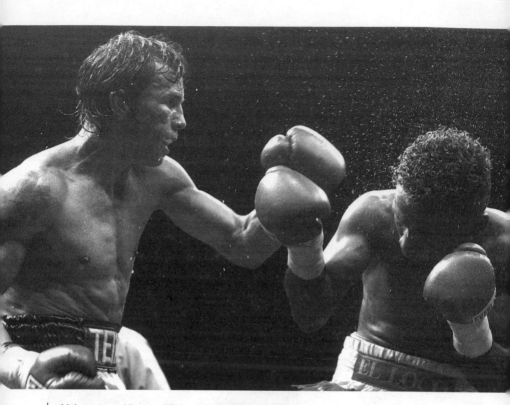

Valero stuns Vicente "El Loco" Mosquera during their WBA super-featherweight title fight in Panama City on August 5, 2006. Valero won the title by technical knockout in the tenth round.
Teresita Chavarria/AFP/Getty Images

Valero celebrates his victory versus Michael Lozada to retain the WBA super-featherweight title at Ariake Coliseum in Tokyo on January 3, 2007. After experiencing years of anonymity in Venezuela, he was now a superstar there.
The Asahi Shimbun/Getty Images

Valero throws a right hand at Nobuhito Honmo
during their WBA super-featherweight fight at
Ariake Coliseum on May 3, 2007. Valero won by
technical knockout in round nine. Honmo never
fought again. *Toshifumi Kitamura/AFP/Getty Images*

After beating Honmo, Valero hugs his son Edwin Jr., who is holding a doll of Venezuelan President Hugo Chavez. *AP Photo*

Valero strikes challenger Takehiro Shimada with
a left cross during another successful defense
of his WBA super-featherweight belt. It was
Shimada's first stoppage loss. *Toru Yamanaka/AFP/
Getty Images*

forced New York officials to recognize that a boxer who wasn't licensed in the state couldn't be suspended. Valero had never been granted a New York license in the first place. A door seemed to burst open as if Valero had kicked it in himself.

In mid-February of 2008, Valero went to Texas and passed the state requirements for a boxing license.

"Thank you to the officials who made this possible and to all the fans who have supported me," Valero said. "I will make you proud."

He brought Jennifer, Edwin Jr., and Roselyn to live in a rented two-bedroom condo in a posh Las Vegas neighborhood. They owned a pit bull and a poodle. The Valero clan could sometimes be seen rolling around town in Edwin's fluorescent yellow Hummer.

People in show business hire entire staffs to create the look of casual glamor that Edwin and Jennifer had quite naturally. They were new-century South American swank. The kids were at the height of their adorableness, like mini-versions of Edwin and Jennifer. And there was Jennifer. She'd grown into a very beautiful woman. To outsiders, Edwin and Jennifer were young and in love and it all seemed effortless.

Earlier in the year, on January 5 at the cathedral of El Vigia, Edwin and Jennifer were officially married. They'd been part of a civil ceremony years earlier, but this was an event that brought the entire family together in a Catholic church. It was the sort of big wedding that Jennifer had dreamed about since she was a girl. She wore a tiara and a breathtaking wedding gown. "She was a very simple girl," recalled a cousin, Dianyeli Viera. "She did not like to put on makeup with strong colors, and that's how it was until her wedding dress: simple."

It was an idyllic time, as Edwin Jr. would say years later. He remembered a day when Edwin and Jennifer played a trick on his sister and him. It started when his parents denied them entrance to the room they usually played in. "After an hour . . . they had the room decorated with many stuffed animals, toys, chocolates of all kinds, and thousands of sweets. They hugged us and said: 'Surprise!' . . . We spent a whole month eating sweets."

Valero seemed like a doting dad. The only problem was that he was restless. He wanted action.

With an American fight in his sights, Valero lurked ringside in Las Vegas when Pacquiao met Juan Manuel Marquez in March 2008. It was the third meeting between Pacquiao and Marquez. Valero correctly predicted a Pacquiao victory by decision, but he was clear about his reasons for being there.

"I have to see my prey close at hand," he said. "They know I can beat them and that's what worries them."

By now Valero was training at the Top Rank gym in Las Vegas, just west of the Strip. Kenny Adams marveled at how sparring partners who were padded up with headgear and puffy, sixteen-ounce gloves still dropped before Valero. In six months, ten sparring partners had decided there were better ways to make a living.

"He'd make them cry," Coyne said. "I'm not exaggerating. Grown men—professional fighters—would cry. Edwin wasn't being an asshole. He just figured they were getting paid, and he would get his money's worth. He wasn't wired to take it easy on people. He was a fucking savage."

When Oscar De La Hoya announced he was returning to boxing to take on Pacquiao, he hired Valero as a sparring partner. After two days, Valero was sent home. Kenny Adams said De La Hoya's team wanted no part of Valero. "I remember his brother saying, 'Kenny, get this monster out of here.'"

De La Hoya had been away from the ring for many months and simply couldn't handle Valero's intensity. It was an omen. Pacquiao beat De La Hoya badly and won by a TKO. Pacquiao became boxing's newest star. De La Hoya promptly retired and went back to promoting.

In December, along with Barrera and welterweight David Diaz, Valero traveled to the Philippines to attend Pacquiao's thirtieth birthday party. It was a gala event in General Santos City, loaded with local politicians and sports figures. The main party included a Las Vegas theme with gigantic playing cards bearing Pacquiao's image.

Valero wore a black suit and tie, looking every bit the well-dressed star, and mingled with some of the top names in boxing. He seemed very pleased with himself, but his cruel humor couldn't be contained. He and Diaz found themselves at a cockfight on opposite sides of the pit. As they readied to release their birds, Valero threw his directly into Diaz's face. Diaz barely missed getting spurred in the eyes.

The big talk of the weekend, however, was Pacquiao's win over De La Hoya. Pacquiao's victory pleased Valero. According to the boxing scuttlebutt, a little feud had erupted between Valero and De La Hoya. The beef stemmed from Valero having given De La Hoya a black eye in sparring, only to learn that De La Hoya claimed another fighter had given it to him. To Valero, this was an incredible sign of disrespect. He was so insulted he vowed to never sign with Golden Boy Promotions.

"Never, never, never," said Valero. "I will not fight under his group."

De La Hoya's blackened eye had an upshot: It gave Bob Arum a chance to get in on the act.

• • •

It was announced in February 2009 that Valero had signed with Top Rank, the legendary promotional company that had been behind some of the biggest fights in history. Arum, Top Rank's cofounder and CEO, had promoted boxing since the 1960s. He helped dozens of fighters become famous, including De La Hoya, Mayweather, and Pacquiao. His greatest quote: "Yesterday I was lying. Today I'm telling the truth."

"Edwin Valero is one of the most exciting fighters in the world today," Arum said, beating the drum for his new find.

Japanese contacts had warned Top Rank that Valero was a problem. He drank a lot. He used drugs. He did as he pleased. But whatever Arum knew, he kept secret. Besides, Valero had impressed Arum as polite and "kind of funny."

And so it was that Arum appeared at Valero's side for his next bout, a Golden Boy Promotions event in Austin, Texas. The opponent was Antonio Pitalua, a durable thirty-nine-year-old veteran of forty-nine contests. Valero promised it would be "a fight to the death."

Colombian-born Pitalua had the wavy hair and pencil mustache of a 1940s Latin bandleader. He also had the rawboned physique of a born puncher, and had accumulated forty knockout wins to prove it. Pitalua's biggest selling point was a recent victory over José Armando Santa Cruz, one of the few fighters to hold his own against Valero in gym sessions. Beating Santa Cruz had earned Pitalua the WBC's rather meaningless "interim" title.

Pacquiao had recently abandoned the WBC lightweight title to seek his fortunes in a higher weight class. Valero and Pitalua would fight for Pacquiao's discarded belt.

Of more interest than the title was the condition of Valero's brain. When asked about his old injury, he bristled, telling one reporter, "It wasn't like they operated on me and took my brain out, washed it off, and put it back in my skull."

The importance of the event meant more interviews than usual. Brian Harty, still compiling footage of Valero for Maxboxing videos, recalled Valero's demeanor with one word: "intense."

"He was always very friendly, always greeted us enthusiastically, always gracious in interviews, but I found him a little unnerving," Harty said. "Sometimes in interviews he could be very mellow, and then sometimes he would get very animated and talk very fast, using his fists for emphasis. The last time I saw him was at another media day in a small LA gym. I was there with Gabriel Montoya, who was interviewing Valero for the first time. In the actual workout, Valero was just crushing a heavy bag and the local fighters were like 'holy shit.' The place shook every time he threw a hook.

"Valero was especially amped up that day. He was shirtless and had the Chávez tattoo, and I don't think he took his eyes off Gabriel or blinked the entire time. His teeth were also kind of jagged, and during the questions and translations his mouth would hang open a little, so for me the impression was like a hungry wolf who was either going to answer your next question or bite you. When it was over, Valero gave Gabriel a handshake like they'd just been through a war together, and I just remember Gabriel turning away sort of dazed and going 'Jesus. . . .'"

Valero broke camp only briefly to get to Venezuela and vote in an election, and then take part in a tribute to the national soccer team at the Miraflores Palace. Then it was back to America for training. It was a hectic time. Valero was fighting stateside for the first time in years, with the expected press commitments involved. Distractions appeared: Ricky Hatton's camp approached Valero with an offer to help Hatton prepare for his own bout with Pacquiao. Valero, probably tired of being Pacquiao's stand-in, turned the offer down. There was also a problem with Pitalua's visa, which nearly caused the bout's cancelation. Finally, Golden Boy Promotions moved in to re-sign Valero. He ignored them. "I think they tried to intimidate me," Valero said, "but they did not succeed."

The fight, which took place on April 4, 2009, at the Frank Erwin Center, had the flair of a Golden Boy promotion. The real Golden Boy stamp was in the form of Robert Alcazar, the man who had trained De La Hoya for many years and was now training Valero. Valero's new manager, Jose Castillo, was allegedly behind replacing Kenny Adams with Alcazar. Valero had wanted a Spanish speaker in his corner.

"He was one of the biggest punchers I've ever seen in my life," Alcazar said in a 2012 YouTube clip. Valero and Alcazar worked together in a private gym in Costa Mesa, California. During the last day of training for Pitalua, Alcazar asked Valero to show him he was ready. Valero proceeded to knock out three consecutive sparring partners. "He possessed a special punch," Alcazar said. "A natural power I've never seen in anyone else. I cannot describe the power in his hands."

The bout was a pay-per-view event with veteran Barry Tompkins calling the action from ringside, with Bernard Hopkins and Doug Fischer providing additional commentary. The trio's services were not needed for long. Valero blew Pitalua away at 0:49 of round two. When the referee stopped the bout, Pitalua fell into his arms.

Tompkins, left breathless by Valero's performance, told the viewing audience, "Every now and then in the sport of boxing you see somebody come along and you'll say, 'That's a guy that's got the goods.' I felt that way about Manny Pacquiao, and I feel that way about this guy."

More recently, Tompkins reiterated that he considered Valero "special. I've always put a lot into how a guy can finish and I thought at the time that he was one of the best I'd seen. If he hurt you—you were gone. Limitless future, I thought."

Nothing in Valero's demeanor suggested there might be a limit to that future.

"Personally I wasn't able to cull much insight as to his personality— mostly because of the language barrier in our meetings," Tompkins said. "He was all business to be sure, but I've seen that dark side in other fighters who weren't like that outside the ring. Apparently, he was dark at all times."

Valero promised to destroy Marquez, Pacquiao, Hatton, or anyone else who got in his way.

"This is the beginning of big things," Valero said. "No man can take my punch."

Arum stood beaming next to Valero, visions of superbouts dancing in his head. "I think he's the best lightweight in the world," said Arum.

An official presented Valero with the WBC lightweight belt. He gave it a quick kiss.

In twelve months, he'd be dead.

• • •

When Valero entered the ring to face Pitalua, he sported a bright new tattoo on his chest. It was a colorful likeness of Hugo Chávez on the Venezuelan flag. There was also the slogan "Venezuela de verdad," which translates loosely to "The true Venezuela." It was the sort of madcap gesture that guaranteed Valero would stick in your memory—that is, if you weren't impressed by an undefeated lightweight whose hands were as heavy as cinder blocks.

Valero got the tattoo in Las Vegas. He'd often worn Chávez's image on his trunks, but the Texas boxing commission had asked him to not wear it for the Pitalua fight. Chávez, after all, had insulted America many times during his presidency. Valero agreed to wear trunks with his country's colors. He added a mouthpiece with his country's colors too. Then, out of spite, he had the tattoo put on his chest. There would be no doubt about where he was from. He'd grown increasingly pro-Venezuela since his friendship with Chávez. "I think we have everything here," he said. "It's the most beautiful place in the world."

His connection to Chávez had deepened since their first conversation in 2006. Chávez had presented Valero with Venezuela's National Hero Award, proclaiming him part of a "golden generation." From then on, Chávez often invited Valero to events he was hosting, and they'd pretend to spar for the cameras. Valero had also been a frequent guest on *Hello President*, the television show where Chávez visited with famous supporters, usually through a video link to the person's home. Sometimes Jennifer appeared at his side.

As delighted as Valero was to be friendly with his president, he became a marked man in the media. He became known as Chávez's fighter. It wasn't a compliment. Venezuela's economy was crumbling, and many in the country blamed Chávez. Yet Valero believed Chávez was a powerful advocate for the poor and oppressed. He sometimes argued with reporters, talking about his part in the "revolution," defending his "commander," describing the sadness he felt while being forced to fight outside of his country.

It was a big change from the fellow who had been frightened of being famous, unsure if Venezuela was safe. Now he said he'd never leave the country, even if Chávez banned professional boxing.

"I'd rather be here in my homeland," he said, "where I'm going to die."

• • •

Valero returned to Venezuela like a prodigal son.

He bought the house he'd been born in. He arranged for the ramshackle farmhouses of Bolero Alto to be outfitted with cable TV and talked about buying new ambulances for El Vigia and setting up neighborhood sports leagues. He invested in properties. He'd host endless parties and dance wildly to peasant music.

Jennifer's young brother Yoel wanted to box, so Valero taught him the basics and encouraged him to fight in the streets. Valero liked to show his fists off—they were covered in little scars and teeth marks, remnants of his own street-fighting career.

Strangely, Valero chose to live in Caracas, one of the most dangerous cities in the world. He could have found a safer spot but opted for a city where the poor scrounged for food, the wealthy traveled in armored cars, and the murder tallies released by the government were slightly below that of a war zone.

Being in Caracas meant reporters from *El Nacional* and other publications had access to him. He was a good talker—glib, frank, and occasionally cryptic. He would talk about his favorite snack (plantains with butter and cheese) or the way his "cold-blooded" nature helped him prepare for fights. He entertained journalists with tales of his rough childhood and gave longwinded monologues about his love of Venezuela.

Mostly, he talked about his children. Though he tended to be secretive about his family in the past, he mentioned them often now. It was as if, now that he had a rapt audience, he was trying to project himself as a good father and family man. "The most important thing is my wife and my children; they are my life. I'm not interested in money; I'm not interested in anything more than my children. The affection that maybe I did not receive, I give it to my children," he said.

Valero was also frank about his old head injury. He knew that someday a doctor might find more problems. If so, he'd retire. "It's my passion," he said, "but I do not want to die in the ring."

Valero began spending his free time at a Caracas bar called The Hangar. He'd drink himself stupid.

He lashed out at people. At family gatherings he could be kind and polite, but a minor comment from someone could set him off. There were more arrests: assaulting a cop; reckless driving; carrying an unregistered gun. The family was concerned about his growing interest in weapons. They told him he was too drunk and irresponsible to have such items. He yelled. He raged. No one could tell him anything.

Then there was a strange incident shortly after the bout with Pitalua. According to Valero, a mysterious assailant drove by his home and fired a shot. It hit Jennifer in the left leg. The wound wasn't serious.

She was out of the hospital in a short time.

• • •

Pacquiao's name kept coming up. There was even an urban legend that Valero had once sparred with Pacquiao at the Wild Card Gym in Hollywood. Freddie Roach, Pacquiao's trainer, even went on record saying Pacquiao handled Valero with no trouble.

The phantom event may be nothing more than wishful thinking that somehow turned into a myth. The occasional fan appeared on boxing forums, insisting he knew someone who was there when Pacquiao and Valero sparred. But it's unlikely that such an encounter would have happened without being caught on video or, at the least, on a camera. Valero was a wily self-promoter and would have made sure there was an audience. He wouldn't spar Pacquiao in an empty gym. As Doug Fischer remembers, Roach "wouldn't let Valero near Pacquiao."

Valero was often asked about Pacquiao in interviews, but he never mentioned this impromptu sparring session. If it had happened, he would have crowed about it.

At times, Valero admitted he needed more experience before tangling with Pacquiao. At other times, Valero was less self-effacing. "Pacquiao is afraid of me," Valero told a reporter for *el Nueva Herald*. "He's been avoiding me for years."

Valero also had great respect for Pacquiao. From cruel poverty himself, Pacquiao was the ultimate rags-to-riches story. Valero's manager, Jose Castillo, saw firsthand Valero's desire to fight Pacquiao. "His dream was to fight Manny," said Castillo. "He went to the Philippines to celebrate Manny's birthday in 2008 and saw how Manny is loved by the people. Edwin wanted that same love."

Edward Valero knew how important such a match-up would be for his brother. "He would tell me that he knew exactly how to catch Pacquiao with his punches. He would show me the movements of how he would step back and around and throw the punches. It meant a lot to him."

Unfortunately, beating De La Hoya had rocketed Pacquiao to a new level. He was *big*. *Time* magazine slotted him at number 13 of the 100 most interesting people of the year. He was now in a position where he was only fighting other big names, such as the Puerto Rican sensation Miguel Cotto. That meant Valero had to wait. No matter how many Venezuelans he pissed off with his tattoo, Valero was merely a cult figure in America, and a minor one at that. Pacquiao was also moving up in weight, keeping a good eight pounds between himself and Valero.

In the spring of 2009, Valero talked as if a Pacquiao bout was a done deal. It was alleged that his contract with Arum had a special clause that said the fight had to be made. The plan was for Valero to fight Umberto Soto in Las Vegas on the undercard of Pacquiao–Cotto, which would introduce Valero to a vast audience.

To Arum's irritation, however, Valero ran into visa trouble. Valero claimed the problems started when a doctor noticed his Chávez tattoo.

The authorities told a different story. The visa was denied because Valero had been popped in Texas for drunk driving and carrying an unlicensed firearm. Valero said the cops who pulled him over were looking for money. They only arrested him when he'd refused to be extorted. The story might have worked in Venezuela, but not in America.

In September, the police were called to the home of Valero's mother. Valero had accused his younger brother Luis of being in love with Jennifer. Windows were smashed, and the neighbors were alarmed by the sounds of broken glass. Valero allegedly smacked his mother and sister and left the house. The El Vigia police found Valero sitting in a van with his Venezuelan manager Segundo Lujano and another friend. Valero was arrested. He denied having hit anyone. His mother released an official statement. She denied any violence had taken place. Valero claimed the whole thing was just a result of his celebrity. He said he'd become a target for people who wanted to wind him up.

He needed a fight.

If he couldn't appear on a Pacquiao undercard, another way to create interest in a possible bout with Pacquiao was to match Valero with one of the Filipino star's previous opponents. Lucky for all involved, Hector Velazquez, a Mexican journeyman who had fought Pacquiao in 2005, was still active in 2009.

• • •

Velazquez was a veteran of more than sixty fights. He looked hard. He had the thick black eyebrows of a cartoon villain. But if fighting Velazquez was supposed to bolster Valero's image, it didn't.

The fight took place on December 19, 2009, in La Guaira, Venezuela. It was messy. Velazquez knew the tricks of survival. He hugged. He butted. It was a damned saloon fight. Valero dug in for a long night. By the fifth round he was landing bombs on the older guy's chin. Velazquez didn't come out of his corner for the seventh. Valero, bleeding from the nose and scalp, said the fight was tougher than he thought it would be.

The internet yawned. Valero was overrated. He was nowhere near Pacquiao's class.

But a bad performance was the least of Valero's problems. His family was concerned about his cocaine habit. His brother Luis took to rifling

43

through Edwin's clothing to see if he could find anything incriminating. He found nothing.

Jennifer was behaving strangely, too. Edwin wasn't sure where he wanted to live, so they rented a small apartment in the Montalban section of Caracas. The children were usually left with a relative. One afternoon, neighbors saw Jennifer on the roof of the building; she fainted and nearly fell off. An ambulance was called. Jennifer had taken an overdose of sedatives. She admitted it was a suicide attempt. She'd been upset because of Edwin: Not only was he abusive, but he had been unfaithful many times.

Eloisa showed up and saw that the apartment was a hovel of empty bottles and horrid odors. Jennifer told Eloisa that Edwin made her take drugs.

The couple enrolled in a rehab clinic in Caracas, but Valero didn't like it. He preferred sitting at home in the dark.

"I don't think he got heavily into the drugs until the last two years," said Fischer. "Back in 2004, that guy was clean and focused. He trained every day, even during his suspension. A promoter could've called him for a championship fight, given him two weeks, and he'd be ready. And he'd win. But by 2008 or 2009 he was making money and he was back in Venezuela. Being out of the country was hard for him, but being back in Venezuela was bad. I'm sure that's when the real drug use started."

There'd also been friction between Valero and Arum.

Arum was frequently dropping Valero's name in public, hinting that he and Pacquiao would fight soon in Japan or China. In private, Arum told Valero that he needed more exposure. Arum suggested possible opponents, but Valero would scoff. He wanted big money and big opponents. He was tired of being a novelty act for hipsters. He wanted Las Vegas, casino perks, high rollers, and movie stars. He wanted a fight that would be mentioned somewhere besides online forums at 2 a.m.

"He was totally erratic," Arum said years later. "He was kind of a nice guy, but then he could go off at any time. He wasn't normal."

Meanwhile, Valero's American contacts found it increasingly difficult to reach him in Venezuela, as if a wall of secrecy had gone up around him. The question was whether Valero would implode before he could become boxing's next bankable star.

Valero's brother Edward had a conversation with Edwin around this time. Drunk and rambling, Edwin told his older brother that he would prefer to see one of his loved ones dead than to face death himself.

"He was very afraid of death," said Edward.

• • •

Antonio DeMarco was next. And last.

February 6, 2010: Monterrey, Mexico. On paper it was a good matchup. DeMarco was a talented twenty-four-year-old from Los Mochis who had won twenty-three of twenty-five bouts, plus a WBC "interim" belt. He was Valero's opposite: He was boyish. He laughed when reporters asked questions. DeMarco was one of those unusual fighters who went about his work happily. He was a tall left-hander who could box and move. Valero would be forced to work harder than usual.

Prior to the bout, Valero presented a calm, thoughtful front. "I'm sure I'm in the best moment of my career," he said at a press event in Monterrey. "This is a sport with a short career and I do not plan to waste it. I want to give the best of me; I want to do many things, leave my best legacy, do important things. I want to be a solid champion and keep climbing. I aspire to great things. . . ."

The fight aired in America on Showtime. American boxing fans who hadn't seen Valero on Spanish television or on grainy YouTube clips would finally see what the hype was about. The Showtime crew was especially fascinated by Valero, including ringside commentator Al Bernstein.

"I knew he had a colorful history, but the interactions with him we had were not in any way difficult," Bernstein remembered. When he shared an elevator ride with Valero prior to the bout, Bernstein was treated to a quick glimpse of the fighter's persona.

"I'll end it quick," Valero said. "I'm a fucking machine."

But it didn't end quickly.

DeMarco boxed beautifully in the first round. He was loose. He glided around the ring. Valero looked at him like a feral dog eyeing his first human. His hair was longer and nastier than ever; he wore a wispy growth of whiskers on his chin. He looked like a mad goat from El Vigia.

In the second, an errant elbow from DeMarco grazed Valero's forehead. The impact opened a dreadful gash, as long and deep as a child's finger. Blood poured out until the right side of Valero's face was a sheet of red. After a momentary stop in the action so a ringside doctor could examine him, Valero charged at DeMarco, throwing his left. The younger fighter did all he could to avoid being decapitated.

The rest of the bout followed in this manner. Valero stalked, DeMarco backed up. With each round, Valero's confidence grew. At some points he was landing three or four consecutive lefts. Sometimes he threw it straight; sometimes he threw overhand, like a street kid hurling a brick through a store window. DeMarco occasionally regrouped long enough to throw some good punches. Valero took them and kept coming forward. He was a snarling mass of hair and blood.

Though he looked the worse for wear, he was creating a kind of masterpiece. He wasn't only bombarding DeMarco with power punches, he was also digging back into his own past, showing the smooth gym fighter he'd once been, the one Joe Hernandez had deemed "an artist." He was slipping and blocking, not letting DeMarco connect on that revolting cut. Being mindful of an injury, and defensive enough to protect it while throwing his thunderbolts, was proof that Valero was not just a mindless slugger. He was, perhaps, special.

"His performance against DeMarco was superb," said Bernstein. "I made a comparison to Manny [Pacquiao]—who was then thought of as best pound for pound—though of course I pointed out [Valero] was not yet on that level—but he reminded me of Manny."

When the ninth round ended, DeMarco walked tiredly to his corner. He slumped onto his stool. He looked as if he'd been hollowed out and tossed aside. His handlers stopped the fight, perhaps at DeMarco's request. DeMarco would tell Showtime's Steve Farhood, "It wasn't my night."

Valero, now 27-0 with twenty-seven knockouts, was hoisted into the air by one of his cornermen and paraded around the ring. He waved a Venezuelan flag and howled. The tableau was one he might have created himself in his dreams—part blood-soaked warrior, part political totem. It was the last time he'd be seen in a boxing ring.

"I remember thinking after that fight that he was going to potentially be a genuine star in the sport," said Bernstein.

Valero would soon inform the WBC that he didn't want the lightweight title. He'd dump it to chase Pacquiao in a higher weight division. The WBC would call him "champion in recess."

DeMarco recovered and had a nice career. He would say God put Valero in his path to test him. He said "no scenario or any rival can put fear in me thanks to that fight."

Inadvertently, DeMarco did something important for Valero's legacy. The elbow in the second round that sliced Valero's forehead gave Valero an everlasting image. In the coming months, as his photograph appeared in endless articles, it was almost always a photo of a bloodied Valero, his eyes glaring through a mask of red, the claret streaming down his chest onto his famous tattoo.

This was the visage we would equate with Valero, the killer.

Carnage

"When I woke up, she was dead,"
—Edwin Valero

The chaos began after the DeMarco bout.

"When Edwin came from Mexico after his last fight, he went crazy," said Edward. "He was drinking and acting strange and wanted to fight with everybody. Cocaine makes you paranoid."

Holy Week was near. The country's bicentennial celebration was weeks away. Valero didn't care. He stayed drunk. He scowled. He accused his brothers of trying to hump his wife.

"Once I went up to the house and his wife was excited to see me and he got mad—he had to be calmed down," said Edward. "His obsession with Jennifer was so strong that it bothered him even when his father or brother would give her a kiss. He would say that Jennifer was his and that she belonged to him."

Jealousy dug into Valero's mind like spurs.

"Edwin was a great person, but the drugs drove him crazy, made him see strange things. He always believed people wanted to hurt him," Edward said.

He wasn't eating or sleeping. He stayed up all night, zooming on drugs and alcohol, creating nightmare scenarios in his mind. He and

Jennifer never left the apartment. Valero's sister Saida visited him around this time. "It was horrible," she said. The champ was hallucinating and believed his mother was in charge of a plot against him.

"He thought we wanted to hurt him, that we wanted to kill him," Saida recalled.

"You're all going to pay for this," he said.

On March 20, Jennifer was admitted to the University Hospital of Los Andes, in the city of Mérida. She had two fractured ribs, perforation of the pleural membrane of both lungs, bruises on the thorax, and a deep bite mark on her back.

Several family members, including Edwin, followed the ambulance in Eloisa's car. Edwin feared people would blame him for Jennifer's injuries. When the car stopped at a red light, Edwin said he had to make a phone call. He got out of the car and ran away. The family went on without him.

On March 25, after not being seen for five days, Valero barged into the hospital and demanded to see Jennifer. Doctor Indira Briceño and nurse Rosa Omaira Zerpa denied him access. Valero said he would have everyone fired if they didn't cooperate. He made threats. He approached Jennifer, held his index finger to his eyebrows, miming a gun. He yelled something in Japanese.

When Valero realized the doctors had called an attorney to open a spousal abuse case, he began to raise hell in the hospital corridors. Hospital staff asked him to calm down but he didn't. The police were called, and Valero argued violently with the arresting officer, threatening to hit him. They got him to calm down long enough to bring him to the Mérida State Police station. He tested positive for cocaine, alcohol, and a prescription muscle relaxer, benzodiazepine. Three days later he was taken to the Criminal Judicial Circuit of Mérida. With Judge Heriberto Peña presiding, Valero was given a closed hearing.

Jennifer was there. Valero greeted her with kisses and they spoke briefly, in whispers.

Jennifer didn't testify against him. She said the cracked rib was caused when she'd fallen down a staircase. The bruises and bites had been caused by a woman who had tried to rob her. Family members verified her story. The judge asked Jennifer if Valero was ever violent with her. She said no. She said they had discussions, no different than other couples, and that the media portrayed her husband as a ruffian.

The beleaguered doctor and nurse held nothing back. They told the judge how Valero had barreled through the hospital, verbally and physically intimidating the staff.

The trial lasted more than three hours, during which time Valero confessed to using cocaine.

Peña ordered Valero be admitted to the San Juan de Dios Psychiatric Hospital in Mérida for six months of treatment and observation. Valero was also ordered to appear in Pena's court every ninety days, and to undergo sensitivity training at the Merideño Institute for Women and the Family. In the meantime, Valero was to remain under police custody and to stay away from Jennifer.

Edwin and Jennifer left the court together. They held hands.

Reactions were mixed. Valero got off easily. Jennifer hadn't even spoken to a psychologist, which might have revealed something about her state of mind.

The news hit America. Valero's admirers winced. Chatroom vigilantes roared. They didn't understand why Jennifer's family let the dirty bastard live.

Three days later, at 10 a.m., a police escort took Valero to the San Juan de Dios Hospital. The collar of his leather coat was pulled up. His hat was pulled down. His face was partly covered by a white surgical mask. Valero looked like a criminal trying to avoid photographers. It was the classic "perp" walk, something Valero probably remembered from his days as a motorcycle punk.

Onlookers outside the hospital jeered. They mocked Valero for being a wife beater. One man shouted, "Pacquiao is going to fuck you up!"

Even at this low point in Valero's life, Pacquiao's name was in the air. Valero gave the crowd the finger.

• • •

Psychiatrist Javier Piñero Alvarado drew the assignment. He diagnosed Valero as "unstable and impulsive." There was a history of brain trauma, plus a "moderate degree of dependence" on drugs. Valero's favorites included marijuana, cocaine, heroin, ecstasy, and crack. There was a "daily frequency for the consumption of cocaine and alcohol in variable quantities greater than ten grams." Alvarado recommended "supervised rehabilitation in a specialized center." The gist: Valero was messed up and needed help.

Valero wasn't under psychiatric care for long, though. His lawyer, Nilda Mora, informed the local media that the hospital was ready to discharge Valero after just three days because his "pathology" was of the sort that they couldn't "take care of him there." He was released on April 7, 2010.

It was rumored that the hospital director wanted Valero out because constant visits from his brothers and sisters were creating a disturbance. The Valero family denied this was true. The Valeros also claimed they had met with Edwin's psychiatrist and were told he should be "rehabilitated elsewhere." They allegedly told the hospital that Valero couldn't leave because he was there under a court order, and that only the judge could determine his release.

"(Edwin) told the psychologist that he was a drug addict who needed help because he felt close to madness," said Edward. Valero had been given drugs at the hospital designed to help, but they had no effect. "In fact, my brother goes free after a few days. No one recovers in such a short time. They could not stand him in the hospital and they ordered him out of there."

Jennifer's aunt Esmeralda later said a doctor from San Juan de Dios had told her Valero was schizophrenic. "I do not understand how they released him . . . if he suffered from schizophrenia," she said.

A bail was set in order for Valero to leave the country and seek help elsewhere. The next day, Valero spoke to Jose Castillo.

"Basically, he said that he knew that he needed the help, and that he couldn't be around his wife right now. That he needed to be separated from her."

Castillo claimed Valero knew he was capable of great violence when under the influence of drugs or alcohol. He knew he needed rehab. He felt he should seek help outside of Venezuela to avoid publicity. They discussed how Castillo would deal with the press if Valero went away for a while.

"That's when he started to tell me a little bit about his childhood," Castillo said, "and why he felt that he had these issues." Valero promised Castillo an email detailing his problems. Valero had odd thoughts in his head. He had bad memories that made him want to stay drunk and high all the time.

"I never got the email," Castillo said.

Valero was off to Havana. Almost.

Governor Jorge Luis Garcia Carneiro of Vargas, Venezuela's former Minister of Defense and a Chávez supporter, arranged for Valero to be sent to Cuba's La Pradera Rehabilitation Center, a highly regarded facility associated with Havana's Latin American Medical School.

Castillo agreed to sign a bond and be responsible for Valero's behavior while he was in Cuba. Castillo was counting on a quick rehab stint. A bout in Mexico was being considered for July. The rehabilitation period would include time for Valero to work with his latest trainer, Mario Morales.

His paperwork ready, the path to Cuba cleared, a drunk Valero crashed his car on his way to the airport. According to one story, Valero had been in the custody of guards hired to escort him. He punched them out, took over the car, and sped away. He wanted to see Jennifer again but was too drunk to drive. Reports say he hit five cars.

On April 17, Valero filled his pockets with cash. He bought some cocaine, and rented a blue Toyota Land Cruiser. He ignored the judge's orders and visited Jennifer. He was going somewhere and talked Jennifer into joining him. She packed a suitcase as if going on a long trip.

• • •

The Hotel Intercontinental is perched on a hill overlooking Valencia. In the distance one can see mountains and river mists. It was an elegant place, though it had seen better days. During Chávez's reign, his portrait hung near the entrance.

At 11:39 p.m., Edwin and Jennifer checked in. Other hotel guests saw them in the reception area, talking quietly to each other. Witnesses said they were together in the lobby for two hours. They had turned down the first room offered—Edwin had complained about noise—and may have been waiting for another room to open up. Room 624, located in a quieter section of the hotel, became available. Valero asked hotel security to check under the bed and in the closets to make sure no one was there. The staff searched the room, and then let Valero take a look.

At 5:30 the next morning, Valero appeared at the front desk. Two versions of the story emerged. In one he was barefoot, "covered in blood." He calmly announced that he had killed his wife. Yet another report described him looking clean, as if he'd had a bath. In this version, Valero nervously paced the lobby with a cup of coffee in his hand. The receptionist asked if a call should be made to see if Mrs. Valero was up. "She won't answer," Valero said. "I killed her."

State troopers arrived at the hotel in thirty minutes. They found Jennifer's body on the floor. There were no signs of struggle. Her throat had been sliced.

Valero went with the troopers peacefully. The photos show him looking weary, not covered in blood at all. He's wearing black track pants, a black and red sleeveless jersey, and a red cap pulled down over his eyes. He's in handcuffs, being escorted by a burly officer. He was taken to the General Command Police Station of Carabobo.

Valero then changed his story. He said gangsters did it. Thugs killed Jennifer.

Jennifer's cousin, Kenya Finol, revealed that Valero had called her from the hotel.

"When he called, he sounded like he was drugged," Finol said. "In a real quiet tone, he said Jennifer was dead in a hotel room in Valencia, and that she had been killed by some thugs who had been pursuing them."

He told a similar story to the police.

Valero's account of the previous night was like a David Lynch movie, full of highways and sinister cops and hotel lobbies crowded with grinning strangers. He described a night of driving and getting high. He swigged vodka, sniffed cocaine. He said he was going to rehab in Cuba, but had lost his passport. He would stay in La Guaira until a new passport was sent to him. He and Jennifer enjoyed the road trip, he said. They were friends again. Then he noticed a car following him. He worried about kidnappers and had stopped at a National Guard checkpoint and asked an officer for help. He claimed the officer told him to go to the Intercontinental. When asked which checkpoint it had been, Valero couldn't remember.

Valero thought Jennifer had given the officer a signal. Valero's brain hummed. Did they want to kidnap him? Once in the hotel, Valero claimed people smiled at Jennifer. A man Valero had never seen before said "hello" to her. Valero was worried that he'd been sent to the hotel as a set-up.

They went to room 624. Jennifer went to sleep, and Valero drank until he passed out.

"I laid next to her," Valero said. "When I woke up, she was dead."

Valero said he had been too high and couldn't remember anything else. He said that he had purchased fifty grams of cocaine in El Vigia. He had snorted so much that his mind was impaired.

Valero turned down a chance to speak to his family. They'd know everything soon enough, he said.

He wanted Segundo Lujano. He told Lujano that the police had taken his suitcase. He said it held $90,000, and that the money should be recovered and given to his children. He wanted to know if his children were safe, demanding to know if someone told them what had happened to their mother. When Lujano told him the children knew, Valero nearly collapsed. "Take care of my children," he told Lujano.

"Now I've screwed up for real," Valero said. "I'll never be able to see my daughter again . . . I'm fucked . . . I need to scrub myself."

Javier Ignacio Mayorca, a reporter from *El Nacional*, was granted an interview; Valero repeated the story of being followed by thugs. "When I saw him he was under the effect of drugs and alcohol," said Mayorca. "Sometimes he had a connection to reality, and sometimes he lost it, but he never confessed to killing his wife."

Valero was taken to a cell. The sight of him stirred the other prisoners. They yowled and banged on their cell doors, whistling and shouting rude things. Hands reached through cell bars to grab at Valero as he passed. Valero looked at the guards as he was being locked in and pleaded with them to stay.

"I feel so alone," he said. "I need to talk to somebody."

They took away his shirt and shoelaces. He was placed on suicide watch.

On April 19, at approximately 1:30 a.m., a prisoner in an adjacent area heard a noise in Valero's cell and called out to the guards. They rushed over to find Valero hanging by the neck. He had used his pants as a noose.

The guards cut him down. Moments later he was dead.

Authorities found a folded paper in Valero's clenched teeth. It was a picture of Valero with his wife and children. Rumors would follow: he'd swallowed his boxing license; he'd swallowed his ID card.

Wilmer Flores Trosel, the general director of Venezuela's largest national police agency, officially announced that the death occurred in Valero's cell. "He used his own clothes, having as support the cell's own grate." Trosel added: "He was encouraged by another inmate to end his life."

By 4 a.m., Valero's body was at the morgue. The toxicology reports said he was loaded to the gills with cocaine.

He'd died on Venezuelan Independence Day.

• • •

There were ghastly revelations. Family members told horror tales about Valero. There was guilt and finger pointing.

Jennifer's uncle, Evelio Finol, said Valero had terrorized the entire Finol family for years. Evelio said they kept quiet about Valero's violent nature because "we were threatened with death." He said Valero had been forcing Jennifer to take drugs since January, "or else he would have killed her, her children, and her mother." During their decade together, "she was always under the threat of death."

Jennifer's family claimed he'd been beating her since she was fourteen. "They were ten years of hell, no love," said Jennifer's aunt Minfa Finol. "She was a very educated and respectful girl, full of values," said Segundo Finol, Jennifer's grandfather, "but her life changed when she joined that monster."

Though Evelio said the Finols were culpable for remaining silent, he also accused the authorities of Venezuela. "Because Valero was an athlete, he received preferential treatment, so they too are responsible for what happened."

Jennifer's father, Armando Viera, said the authorities had ignored his previous pleas for help. "Her mother and I repeatedly told the security forces . . . about El Inca's abuse of my daughter, and they never believed us, now this happens." Armando had often told Jennifer to simply leave with the children, though another relative said, "This would have happened anyway."

Eloisa said her son was ruined by a decade of drug and alcohol abuse. "The authorities of this country are responsible for everything," she said.

"It's true that I have to take the blame for not saying anything, but Edwin was very ill."

"I asked the authorities not to let him out," Jose Castillo said. "He was very bad in the head, beside himself, but they let him out. They were very permissive with him and that's why we are now in the middle of this tragedy."

Castillo insisted Valero "was an extremely good person." He continued: "I know that it is very hard to imagine that, considering the tragedy that just happened. But deep down inside, Edwin was a very caring person. Unfortunately, he had some issues with his childhood and with his past that most people don't know about. Obviously, it must be hard to imagine the feeling he must have been dealing with that would drive him to do this. . . . Being that he was in Venezuela, there were just so many factors. We will never know exactly what was going through his mind these last few weeks and days. It's very tragic, and I would like for the public to kind of think about that. Deep down, he had some issues and he was still a human being."

Castillo added that Edwin was impossible to know. "It's like if you're watching a movie from the middle to the end. You really can't understand why the ending came out that way without watching the beginning, and most people don't know what the beginning of Edwin Valero was."

"He was a street child," said Lujano. "He did not have anything to eat or a place to sleep. He had many depressive problems."

A spokesman for the police admitted that Valero should have been put into a straitjacket and placed in a padded cell. Unfortunately, he said, no such facilities were available.

Jorge Linares, a fellow Venezuelan boxing star, described the murder-suicide as "a hard blow for the sport, for those of us who appreciated him . . . and for all Venezuelans.

"What's important is that we learn a lesson," Linares continued. "We admired him as an athlete, but we never did anything to help him with his problems. We could have started by making public his problems and not hiding anything."

Oscar Ortega, the trainer who had once allowed Valero to sleep in his gym, blamed the people in Valero's crowd. "Those people around him were like piranhas," he said. "They bit him and they did not let him go."

Of course, Hugo Chávez chimed in, too. The president blamed the Venezuelan media "rabble," claiming that a "siege" on Valero had been planned for months. The media had to destroy Valero because he was a political symbol. "Today, like vultures, they feed on the corpses of Jennifer and Edwin."

Anti-Chávez bloggers went loco. To them, Valero was an example of Chavismo run amok. Venezuelan newspaper editors blamed a judicial system cowed by Chávez. Chávez's supporters scolded those who would use a tragedy to make political points. It was like a 1930s Greenwich Village socialist debate, based on the shabby premise of a dumb drug addict who thought his wife was unfaithful. Media stooges made their deadlines and forgot about it. They reached for familiar motifs about fame going to Valero's head. They left the political gaga to the message boards and leaned on tragedy and bewilderment.

Women's groups jumped up. More than one feminist blogger was sickened that Valero was being treated like a national hero, while Jennifer was simply referred to as "his wife." "She was murdered because she was a woman," boomed a statement from a Venezuelan women's foundation, "practically in front of our eyes."

A short time after her murder, middleweight champion Sergio Martinez had his trunks embroidered with Jennifer's name. There was hope that Jennifer's death would bring attention to Venezuela's apathy toward violence against women. Still, the attention remained on Valero. In Venezuela, the tragedy was less about a woman being murdered than about a famous sports figure who had gone berserk.

And then there was José Sulaimán, the head of the WBC. He blamed Valero's downfall on America.

"The United States failed him," Sulaimán said, insisting that Valero's loss of his visa denied him "a great career."

Of course, America couldn't have cared less about the comments of Sulaimán. In Edwin Valero, America had a new bogeyman.

• • •

The major American news outlets gave the story skimpy coverage. They relied on sketchy reports from the Associated Press and Reuters. They played up the wife-abuse angle.

The more intense coverage was online. The internet had made Valero; now it immortalized him as a bug-eyed psychopath who hacked his wife to bits. He was a cocaine snorting Jason Voorhees—Charles Manson with a perfect knockout percentage.

The story was ideal for internet readers who were used to sensationalism and half-assed reporting. There had been the recent suicide of Alexis Arguello and the mysterious death of Arturo Gatti, but this Valero thing was more gruesome. It had horror and hotels, cocaine and stabbing and suicide. Boxing writers in the United States rested on typical angles about concussion syndrome; they pondered steroid rage. They vilified greedy fight promoters who made money as Valero grew crazier. They blamed themselves for supporting such a vulgar, violent pastime. Then they cheerfully gave their predictions for the upcoming Mayweather–Mosley fight. The people on message boards defined the tone. They'd never liked Valero in the first place. The moral of the story seemed to be that you should never trust an overhyped internet phenomenon.

When Jennifer's age was incorrectly given as twenty, rather than twenty-four, web forums exploded. Between that error and bad translations, word got out that Valero had married Jennifer when she was ten. It was nonsense, but it played like Beethoven. The pedophilia angle made the story more disturbing. It was clickbait. Major outlets, including the New York *Daily News,* continued to list Jennifer's age as "either 20 or 24."

Even the most fair-minded coverage was accompanied by photos of Valero from the DeMarco fight, his eyes caught in a moment of blue fury, blood pouring down from the gash on his forehead, his mouth open as if screaming.

Boxing websites went loco. They didn't try to make sense of how a degenerate with mental problems had been left abandoned in a prison cell. They were selling outrage and judgment. They were selling Valero as Jack the Ripper.

• • •

Valero was buried on April 21. The sky was blue enough for a postcard, the kind you might buy at the Hotel Intercontinental, one that would say *Saludos De Venezuela!* It was a funeral worthy of a national dignitary, with three thousand people turning out.

Valero's coffin was taken from his mother's home in El Vigia and transported to his father's house in Bolero Alto. A caravan of trucks and motorcycles blew horns and sirens; some Valero fans simply ran along on foot for as far as they could, shouting "Champion! Champion!"

A service was held in La Palmita. From there it was off to the Rodriguez gym where Valero learned boxing. Jennifer's young brother Yoel showed up in his boxing gear and sparred with a friend in front of the coffin. "He was someone big," Yoel said. "It breaks my heart to see him like that— dead. He still had a lot to give."

The procession then traveled six miles to the Cristo Rey private cemetery on the national highway that leads to San Cristóbal. Onlookers swarmed in and tried to touch the coffin.

Valero received a Christian burial in the company of his closest family members. Eloisa was devastated. The pain in her face, in the photographs from the funeral, is difficult to view. Edwin Jr., crying the whole time, was asked to pose for a picture. He instinctively stood in a fighter's stance.

The coffin was lowered into the ground. People threw flowers in, covering their faces in anguish. Dogs milled around. One dog lay down by Valero's open grave.

Alejandro Martinez, a fan that assisted with the burial, summed up the afternoon.

"I am angry," Martinez said. "He committed a heinous crime. He killed his wife and left his children without a mother, but he is still a champion. He put the name of this town, of Merida, of the country in front of the whole world. His punches, how he fought, it was spectacular. He could have beaten Manny Pacquiao. His attitude, his aggressiveness, he was going to go far in boxing. You can't forget that, two-time world champion, undefeated. He killed, yes, but I applaud him and I cry for him because he was a great athlete."

The cemetery's online tribute section included the usual comments. A woman known only as "Mary" wrote, "A very sad ending for two young people. . . . Rest in Peace, Edwin. See you in Heaven." An anonymous contributor wrote in Spanish, "Look at what your sick fanaticism for Hugo Chávez did, another murderous psychopath like you."

Valero's coffin was draped with the flag of Venezuela. He was buried next to Jennifer.

• • •

It took ten years, but this is where Jennifer landed—on the floor of room 624 at the Hotel Intercontinental.

Crime-scene photos show that she spent the final moments of her life on a worn carpet. Not far from her body is an empty wastebasket, turned on its side. Empty beer cans and liquor bottles are arranged neatly on the floor near the bed. A few small items are on the carpet: a button, a bottle cap, a crumpled wrapper.

She's on her back, her head turned to the right. Her eyes are closed and her arms are at her sides. She wears a brown shirt, pulled up to reveal her stomach. Her blue jeans are unbuttoned and her bare feet are against the wall, crossed as if trying to keep warm.

Her throat is cut. It's a neat job—the gash is dark red, almost black. There are blood smears on her chin, her right shoulder, across the top of her chest, and along the inside of her left arm near the elbow. There is a bloodstain on her right pant leg. A long stain can be seen on the carpet next to her head, perhaps from when the blood sprayed from her.

Three wounds are reported. Only the throat wound is visible.

Her lips are parted. There's a gap in her front teeth. The gap doesn't exist in previous photos, as if there'd been recent damage to her mouth.

Jennifer's unopened luggage can be seen. A couple of detectives are at the edges of the photos—large, well-dressed men wearing heavy black shoes, carrying cardboard pointers.

There are photographs of the unmade bed. The pillows are pushed together in the middle of the mattress. The blanket is shoved down to the bed's lower right corner. A bloody sheet appears to have been yanked from the bed and placed under a table. On the bed is a gray bra.

It is not a frenzied crime scene. This is probably what started the rumor that there had been no blood. There was certainly blood, but not as much as one might think.

She was likely killed on the floor. The carpet stain runs exactly parallel to the cut on her throat.

"The stain on the floor looks clotted," said Amy Brodeur, a forensic science expert from the Boston University School of Medicine who was shown the crime-scene photographs. "There is a heavy amount of blood, but I don't know if it resulted from blood spurting out of her neck or possibly from her bleeding face down and then later rolled over."

It was estimated that Jennifer had been killed at approximately 4 a.m., which meant Valero had been in the room with the corpse for ninety minutes before coming down to the lobby.

Forensic experts ran a luminol test in the bathroom of room 624. They found traces of blood in the sink. There were also blood traces found on a towel. It appeared the towel had just been washed.

There were no reports of a scream. Jennifer may have been killed as she slept.

"There is a fair amount of blood on the bed, the sheets, pillow, and maybe on the bedspread, too. Some of it appears to be from active bleeding, not simply from the killer wiping his hands or the blade," said Brodeur. Jennifer may have been stabbed on the bed and then placed on the floor where her throat was cut. Her positioning is unusual. Her body looks as if it had been placed on the carpet rather gently. She appears "carefully situated," said Brodeur. "So possibly she was positioned."

No murder weapon was found.

The forensic expert who examined Jennifer's body didn't think she was killed with a knife as the wounds were not deep. They were like the wounds made by a scalpel.

No one could imagine Valero using something as dainty as a surgeon's tool. This added to the belief that someone else had killed Jennifer. It was too neatly done.

Luis Valero said of his brother: "He was so violent when he used drugs that I'm sure that if he had killed her, he would have bitten her into pieces."

• • •

In Venezuela the rumors sailed along like parade floats.

The story had big gaps in it. People felt obliged to fill the gaps with bullshit.

An unnamed tipster contacted a Spanish-language news site and told a tale that involved a grocery store in the San Isidro del Vigia neighborhood. The story was right out of *Reefer Madness*. It went like this: Valero had purchased the store for Jennifer's mother. It served as a front for cocaine dealers. Valero wanted to get Jennifer and the children away from such people, but Jennifer had become a full-blown cokehead. She wanted to stay near her new contacts. Sometimes, high on cocaine, she'd physically attack Valero; he'd have to defend himself. This, according to the informer, is why she ended up in the hospital. Valero never told anyone that Jennifer was an addict. He wanted to keep her name out of the news.

Valero's dread that someone was following him was not a delusion, said the tipster. Drug dealers wanted to settle old scores. Their reach extended into the prison where he died.

The tale was just one example of the gossip that erupted after Valero's death. Nonsensical stories appeared almost daily. They didn't shed much light on the events but served other purposes. First, they allowed the storyteller to be part of what seemed like a national tragedy. And for people not ready to let Valero go, these anecdotes kept him alive for the length of a newspaper column. Ultimately, the gossip was a reaction from people who simply couldn't make sense of what had happened. Any story, no matter how ludicrous, was preferable to Valero murdering Jennifer and then hanging himself in a dungeon.

How Valero actually managed to hang himself was a question. If he was on suicide watch, why didn't the guards get to his cell until he was taking his last breaths? And what about the comment from Trosel that Valero had been "encouraged" by another inmate?

Pictures of Valero's corpse leaked onto the internet. Amateur sleuths figured the tattoo looked wrong. It had to be an imposter. The real Valero was on the lam somewhere in Cuba.

Edward Valero felt there was something shady about his brother's suicide. The pants Edwin allegedly used to hang himself were never produced. There were even conflicting reports about what sort of pants had been used—were they blue jeans or sweatpants? There were bruises on Valero's body and strange bumps on the back of his head. "I think my brother was killed," Edward said.

This wasn't an unlikely possibility. Venezuela's prisons are hellish places where anything can happen, up to and including cannibalism. If Valero's head had a price on it, a couple of guys could have strangled him with his pants and made some money.

The Valero family demanded a new autopsy for Edwin.

On April 29, 2010, Venezuelan Attorney General Luisa Ortega Díaz authorized the exhumation of Valero's remains. On May 13, Valero's body was removed from its grave. In yet another bizarre story, Valero's corpse was apparently decomposed almost beyond recognition, indicating it might not have received proper treatment at the funeral home. Yet the Chávez tattoo was still clearly visible, as if Valero's loyalty to his commander would outlast his own body.

A second autopsy was performed and specialists deduced that the marks on Valero's neck were in keeping with someone who had died by hanging. The wounds on Valero's head came from convulsions when his body was taken down. The conclusion, again, was that he died by hanging or mechanical asphyxia.

Edward Valero didn't accept it. "I went to the headquarters where Edwin supposedly committed suicide and there all the officials had a different version," he said in 2016. "Some say they found him wearing his trousers, others that he was on the floor with his trousers on the floor." The mark on Edwin's neck didn't look like anything made by a fabric. It was, Edward claimed, "as thick as a cable."

Edward also said the case's original prosecutor, Richard Daal, had told him Edwin died not from hanging at all but from a medication that had caused "internal suffocation." Later, Daal "changed that version and said he never told me that."

The official word was that Edwin Valero killed himself. But had he really killed Jennifer?

Valero attacks Mexican challenger Hector
Velazquez while defending his WBA lightweight
world title in La Guaira, Venezuela, on December
20, 2009. Velazquez was a tougher opponent than
expected, but he retired after six rounds. *Nixon
Alviarez/AFP/Getty Images*

Valero and Antonio DeMarco pose together the day before their WBC world-title fight in Monterrey, Mexico, on February 6, 2010. Notice Valero's wild-eyed stare.
Alfredo Lopez/Jam Media/Latin Content via Getty Images

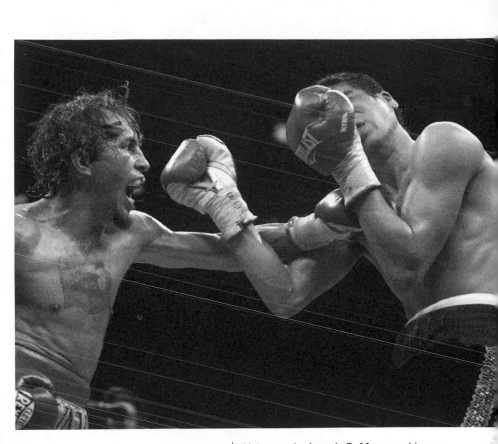

Valero rocks Antonio DeMarco on his way to victory. DeMarco's corner stopped the fight after round nine. *Omar Torres/AFP/ Getty Images*

Part ring warrior, part "Chavista," Valero celebrates his last victory. *Omar Torres/AFP/ Getty Images*

After Edwin's three-hour trial for assaulting Jennifer, she leaves the Merida courthouse. She refused to testify against him. *Archivo Latino*

The crime scene at room 624 in the Hotel Intercontinental in Valencia, Venezuela.

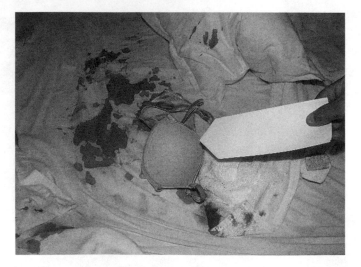

Initial reports said there was little blood in room 624, but this photo shows otherwise.

Valero, after his confession, is escorted to the police station in Valencia. *AP Photo*

Jennifer's brother Yoel spars with a friend as part of Valero's funeral service. *Miguel Gutierrez/AFP/ Getty Images*

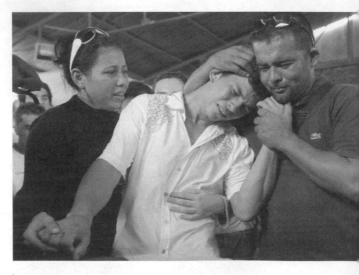

Valero's death was viewed as a national tragedy in Venezuela, as shown by these anguished mourners. *Miguel Gutierrez/AFP/Getty Images*

• • •

Details from the hotel were muddled. Was Valero barefoot and blood spattered, or was he cleaned up, with a cup of coffee? Had he really confessed to the hotel staff? If Valero killed Jennifer, why would he go through the trouble of hiding the murder weapon *and then* confessing?

The Venezuelan media was strapped. Chávez had passed laws preventing reporters from asking questions at murder scenes. Police officers who shared information with the press could be punished. Victims' relatives are asked not to speak with reporters. And just four months after Jennifer's death, a Venezuelan court banned newspapers from printing bloody photos of murder victims. How could anyone investigate the Valero case when asking too many questions could cost you so much?

Valero's admirers weren't satisfied. The most popular conspiracy angles included anything from anti-Chávez crusaders to a botched kidnapping attempt. When word got out that Valero had paid for the room in cash, it was assumed that thieves in the lobby had seen him flashing his money around and decided he was an easy mark. They had killed Jennifer, but when Valero stirred, they bolted from the room.

Did Jennifer resist a kidnapper and end up with a slashed throat? Did police fail to find a murder weapon because someone ran out of the hotel with it?

The police announced they would examine surveillance tapes to see if anyone had entered room 624 while Edwin and Jennifer slept. When the hotel failed to produce the tapes, conspiracy theorists had fits. Was hotel management involved in a cover-up?

The kidnapping theory was hot for a while. Some said Chávez had organized the whole thing. Valero had become an embarrassment to him, so the commander ordered both Jennifer and Edwin killed.

The conspiracy theorists were of a type. The bloggers and commenters were, too. They were angry and political, approaching the story on political terms. They lived politics and talked politics and sincerely believed that the Valero case was just an extension of Venezuela's rock-bottom poverty and discord. They thought that hating Chávez made them capable of solving the crime. Logic meant nothing. Here was a cocaine freak who never slept, yet he slept so soundly that he didn't hear Chávez's goons sneak into the room and kill Jennifer. If Chávez wasn't involved, it had to be a powerful drug lord. Drug dealers loomed large in the Venezuelan psyche, where they were imagined to control everything, even the life and death of a boxing champion.

Perhaps realizing how silly they sounded, the conspiracy lovers eventually calmed down. But Valero's fans never gave up on him. Though outnumbered by Valero's haters, the faithful hit the online forums hard for months. *No way did Edwin kill Jennifer. He loved her too much. She had to have been killed by someone else. . . . If he did do it, he did it out of love. . . .*

The loyalty, though misplaced, was poignant.

• • •

Time passed. Valero dropped out of the headlines.

"El Loco" Mosquera ended up in prison for manslaughter but was later cleared. Pacquiao would have a long, colorful career. He'd earn more than $150 million and be elected to the Congress of the Philippines. He'd appear on *Jimmy Kimmel Live!* and sing "Sometimes When We Touch."

Chávez died. Venezuela's economy nosedived, and the crime rate exploded. The prison where Valero died made news in 2018 when a fire swept through the place, killing more than sixty people.

Jennifer's younger brother Yoel became an acclaimed amateur flyweight, winning a bronze medal at the 2016 Summer Olympics, Venezuela's first boxing medal in thirty-two years. He never says anything negative about Edwin but adds: "I've forgiven him." Edwin's younger brother Luis took up boxing but quit because he didn't have the chops.

Merida newspaper columnists regurgitate the Valero story now and then. There are occasional updates about the children. The government never came through on promises to help, though. The kids were shuffled around to various family members and were told that an intruder killed Jennifer and that Edwin was killed in prison.

José Ramón Contreras Batista, a journalist and former president of the Merida Boxing Association, says Valero is missed in Venezuela. "In these days of crisis that the country is living, his public remembers him," said Batista. "He was the best of the Venezuelan fighters. Currently, the local fans do not see anyone of his stature. So, Edwin has not been forgotten by his fans. On the contrary. As for the tragedy, Valero is remembered as neither a hero nor villain, but as the product of his immaturity, the son of a dysfunctional home."

Others say Valero is not remembered at all outside of boxing circles. Venezuelans have other things to think about.

Edward Valero still carries a torch for his brother. He maintains that Edwin was a kindhearted man who set up a foundation to assist the poor children and the elderly of Merida. "These are things that people should know about Edwin Valero," Edward says. Edward considers the murder of Jennifer an unsolved mystery. "We still don't know what happened," he says, adding that people think too much about the gruesome ending of his brother's life. "It's also a sports story," he once told a reporter. "Let's not forget that."

Eloisa says much of what has been written about her son is untrue. Edwin wasn't using drugs in his childhood, she says. That was an exaggeration he told a doctor. She doesn't know why he would say such a thing.

Eloisa has her own theory about what happened in April 2010. She'd helped her son pack his suitcase before the trip. She knew about the $90,000 and believes he opened the suitcase when he was renting the Toyota, or perhaps when he bought the cocaine. Someone saw that Valero was traveling with cash; the car Valero thought was following him all night was someone he'd done business with that day. Ninety thousand in Venezuela would go a long way. Someone followed Valero with the intention of stealing that money.

The police never returned the suitcase. Eloisa called the authorities many times about it. She had theories and wanted to talk. They wouldn't take her calls.

• • •

Weird tales come out of Venezuela. Valero's prized Ford Mustang sat rusting and unclaimed in a parking lot near Caracas. His money remained tied up in foreign accounts. When Hugo Chávez grew ill with cancer, there was a movement among Chavistas to dig up Valero's grave one more time and remove his tattoo in the belief that it was harming Chávez's health.

In 2016, a guest columnist on an El Vigia website accused the WBC of letting Valero fight while he was high on cocaine. Another Venezuelan columnist openly wondered if Valero had killed others besides Jennifer; yet another feared a dangerous cult might spring up in Valero's memory. There was concern that Valero's actions might inspire copycat killers or copycat suicides.

Unsubstantiated rumors were still hot: a "historian" wishing to remain anonymous claimed Valero used to book hotel rooms for himself and three women, locking in for a weekend of debauchery. He would also wander the streets of his old El Vigia neighborhood at night, a handgun in his belt, like a character in a Charles Bronson drama.

In December 2016, a movie called *El Inca* premiered in Venezuela. The Valero family protested. Supreme Court Judge Salvador Mata Garcia decided the film was an invasion of privacy and could have a bad effect on Edwin Jr. and Jennifer Roselyn, and *El Inca* was gone from theaters in a few weeks.

Filmmaker Ignacio Castillo Cottin had the Valero family's cooperation at first but severed ties when they objected to his screenplay. Cottin's film, done in the overwrought style of Latin American soap operas, shows Valero having a fling with one of Jennifer's friends. Edward Valero declared the movie was "false," nothing more than "yellow journalism." Cottin eventually admitted the film was "fictionalized."

El Inca was eventually made available on Pantaya, an online streaming service for Spanish-language films. The fictionalized story of Edwin Valero therefore became part of an archive that included teen sex comedies, spaghetti westerns, and Mexican movies where masked wrestlers solve crimes.

• • •

In 2017, a team headed by forensic psychologist Carlos Ortiz performed a "psychological autopsy" on Valero. They wanted to reconstruct his life actions to determine what exactly had driven him to take his own life. The murky conclusion, published on *Caraota Digital,* was that Valero's suicide was not driven by depression but "more the impulsiveness that characterized his life."

Vice.com brought up Valero in 2017 during the controversy over the movie. The life of Valero, Cesar Gonzalez Gomez wrote, "continues to confuse the public, which insists on trying to understand it through the lens of normality. But there is little of normality in people like Valero. They do not register compassion or fear, but it is not that they lose touch with those emotions. They just never developed them since they were born." The editorial characterized Valero as charismatic but utterly void of human feelings. "He knew how to seduce. But it is that naturalness for deception that makes people like Edwin Valero dangerous." Gomez's thoughts bring to mind the essential traits mentioned in Sigmund Freud's 1928 description of the criminal psychopath: "absence of love, and lack of an emotional appreciation of human objects."

It's too easy to dismiss Valero as an unfeeling psychopath. Jennifer's aunt Esmeralda claimed a doctor believed Valero was schizophrenic.

Though he hadn't been observed long enough for an official diagnosis, Valero certainly exhibited some schizophrenic behavior, particularly his overreacting to stressful conditions, delusional thinking, the belief that he was being threatened, and his dips into depression.

Valero's extended cocaine use could also create symptoms resembling schizophrenia. Meanwhile, recent studies have revealed that cocaine actually helps relieve the schizophrenic's sense of unease. There's the possibility that, as he aged and the schizophrenic symptoms increased, he may have used cocaine to level himself off. But then the cocaine had its own insidious effects.

The traumatic head injury he endured at nineteen could have caused these symptoms as well. Study the backgrounds of many violent people, including serial killers, and there is almost always a head injury in their past.

Valero believed Jennifer was unfaithful, so it is possible that he felt he had to kill her to relieve his own pain and humiliation. Obsession grows in a person's mind until there's room for nothing else.

If Valero was a womanizer, as many believe, that could have added to his paranoia. He may have feared that Jennifer might be unfaithful just to get even.

The thought of his wife with someone else took root in his mind and festered. He wasn't unfeeling. He felt too much. He felt everything digging at him like thorns.

• • •

The internet is where he remains. It surrounds him like a cheap coat. You might see an "Edwin Valero" autographed boxing glove on an internet auction, going for a thousand dollars or so. An old program from one of his Japan fights might fetch sixty bucks. There are some T-shirts with his likeness, including one in the style of the 1983 *Scarface* movie poster, as if linking Valero to that other coke-snorting killer, Tony Montana.

There was allegedly video footage of Valero dying in prison, frothing at the mouth, but all you might find now are a few drab photos of him on a gray prison floor.

There hasn't been any great rush to rehabilitate his image. There are occasional comments on message boards about "the waste of talent." Some pat themselves on the back and say they never bought into the hype. Mostly, he's remembered as a sicko sadist, a legacy summed up by the title of an online story marking the one-year anniversary of his death: "Edwin Valero: The Homicidal Maniac Who Never Got the Chance to Fight Manny Pacquiao."

Valero was even bumped from *The Guinness Book of World Records,* Tyrone Brunson, a Philadelphia middleweight, racked up nineteen consecutive first-round knockouts against some soft opponents, surpassing Valero's previous record of eighteen.

For now, Valero's presence is strongest on YouTube. Old sparring partners and trainers turn up in videos shot in LA gyms. They verify that he was great. They say he was a harder hitter than Pacquiao. Kenny Adams appeared in one, saying that Valero used to ask for Viagra in order to train. These men don't say much about the sad events of April 2010. These are boxing men; they talk boxing. Adams has doubts about Valero's suicide, though. "I think he was set up," he said.

There are several "Pacquiao–Valero" packages on YouTube. Talking heads offer opinions on how things might have turned out. For some, it's the superfight that got away. Bob Arum has denied there was ever any interest in a Valero–Pacquiao bout. In an example of "yesterday I was lying," Arum said in 2018 that a bout involving Pacquiao and Valero was "never a consideration."

The more sentimental of Valero's fans make commemorative videos about him. They use footage of him in happier times, while gooey music plays in the background.

Best of all are the old fights. When you watch those old clips, you can almost understand the fans who believed they were looking at boxing's next star. At a time when boxers were losing their bigger-than-life aura, Valero seemed an amalgam of the great ones. He was Dempsey. He was Duran. He was Liston. He was Tyson. He wasn't trying to win on points. He was trying to be unforgettable.

His life isn't so hard to understand. It was a madhouse version of childhood angst. Edwin Valero wanted powerful things from the world, but feared he couldn't get them. He reinvented himself like a kid putting on costumes, and was sure he was the strongest fighter alive. He screwed up. He wasn't bright and couldn't see that he was creating his own hell on earth. He trained hard because he was creating his own Frankenstein monster, one born of a childlike fascination with strength. He turned himself into a character that his younger self might have idolized. The new Valero was just the unhappy kid he used to be, but with fighting skill and a body full of drugs. He wanted to be an important figure, but he was still a seven-year-old who had been abandoned. He met a girl he loved. He feared she would abandon him, too, so she ended up dead in a hotel.

Some of the crime-scene photos appeared on sleazy websites. Subscribers left lewd comments about Jennifer's body and complained that there wasn't much gore. Despite the hopes of women's groups, Jennifer's death didn't really do much except to prove that the sight of a pretty young female with a slashed throat is good currency anywhere.

• • •

How do you end such a story? Maybe lambast Venezuela's drug culture or blame boxing and all of its evils. Maybe, like a detective in an old movie, become obsessed with the murdered woman and try to find the real killer.

There's no suitable ending. There's no kiss off. There's no grand statement.

Edwin Valero was a Rorschach test made in blood. You can see in him what you want. He was a drug addict with anger-management problems. He was a street kid who couldn't handle fame. He was a professional fighter who couldn't restrict his violence to the ring. At his simplest, Valero was like one of those hillbilly husbands sometimes found in Southern literature, trying to keep his ignorant child bride locked away from the world. At his most complicated, he was a cauldron of psychological misfires and drug mania.

He'll recede into history. Years from now, when a boxer of the future murders his wife, the public will act like it's never happened before. You'll mention Valero and get vacant stares. Every generation has killers. The ones that came before are just gallery pieces.

That's how it ends. We can't bury the guy again.

• • •

A month after Jennifer's death, her mother Mary invited a Venezuelan reporter into her home. Many aunts and female cousins gathered around. They told stories of Jennifer.

She was a simple girl, with simple tastes. She liked dolls and cartoons. She liked fried meats. She liked crafts. Her nickname was "Carito," or "Caro," short for Carolina, her middle name. The mother said Edwin saw Jennifer on the balcony of her grandfather's house when they were kids, and that's when he decided that he wanted to marry her.

The women didn't speak ill of Edwin. They agreed he was jealous and possessive, but they talked mostly of the better days, how he'd recently taken Jennifer to a major beauty pageant, which thrilled her, and how she'd kept her second pregnancy a secret. She surprised the family when she returned from Los Angeles with a new baby in her arms.

And they laughed about the time Edwin and Jennifer ran off together in his old banana truck. Ten years had passed, but that rusted old heap was still giving the family a laugh. It must've been a real mess, that truck. But those two kids got in it, ready for their big adventure. He'd be a famous fighter. She'd be a famous model. They got in that old truck, the future fueled by dreams. Then they were gone.

SELECTED SOURCES

Many news sources were consulted for this book. They include ABS-CBN News, Aporrea.com, The Associated Press, badlefthook.com, Boxingscene .com, The Boxing Tribune, Buzzfeednews.com, Caraota Digital, Contropunto .com, Dailymail.com, Elespanol.com, elestimulo.com, El Mundo en Orbyt, El Nueva Herald, elnuevodia.com, enelvigia.com, Enlapizarra.com, ESPN.com, ESPN Deportes, Fanhouse Boxing, *The Guardian*, informe21.com, IPSnews .com, Marca.com, Maxboxing.com, Medscape.com meridaaldiasolofotografia .blogspot.com, mysanantonio.com, *The New York Times, The New York Post,* notifight.com, Panorama.com, philstar.com, reportero24.com, Reuters, Ringtv .com, Soloboxeo.com, *Sports Illustrated,* SportsVice.com, ThaBoxingVoice.com, The United Press, Venalogia.com.

Venezuelan Periodicals
Líder, Meridiano, Mundo Frontera, Pico Bolívar

YouTube
The Maxboxing footage of Valero is available in various forms on YouTube. It is highly recommended, if only to see a different side of Valero than was seen in his fights. One can also find interviews with Robert Alcazar and Kenny Adams where Valero is discussed.

Author interviews
Al Bernstein, October 30, 2018
Steve Farhood, October 30, 2018
Barry Tomkins, November 11, 2018
José Ramón Contreras Batista, November 13, 2018
Amy N. Brodeur, M.F.S., F-ABC, November 17, 2018
Brian Harty, December 5, 2018
Douglass Fischer, December 15, 2018
Ryan Coyne, December 16, 2018

Special thanks to Nancy Van Tine, Esq., and Carlos Cuevas, PhD, for their insight into domestic violence.

Sarah Collins's 2013 article, "The Schizophrenia-Cocaine Link: Breaking the Cycle" can be found on the NYU Steinhardt website.

Several people in Venezuela were contacted for this project. They didn't respond.

ABOUT THE AUTHOR

Don Stradley is an award-winning writer whose work has appeared in various publications, including *The Ring*, *Ringside Seat*, and ESPN.com. Along with his boxing coverage, he's written about baseball, NASCAR, and professional wrestling. Past books include *Schooled*, a dual biography of Lebron James and Jim Morris for Scholastic, and a chapter in *The Ultimate Book of Boxing Lists* by Bert Sugar and Teddy Atlas. When not writing about sports, he's written about the movies for such magazines as *Cinema Retro* and *Noir City*.

Berserk is set in 9.5-point Palatino, which was designed by Hermann Zapf and released initially in 1949 by the Stempel foundry and later by other companies, most notably the Mergenthaler Linotype Company. Named after the sixteenth-century Italian master of calligraphy Giovanni Battista Palatino, Palatino is based on the humanist typefaces of the Italian Renaissance and reflects Zapf's expertise as a calligrapher. Copyeditor for this project was Shannon LeMay-Finn. The book was designed by Brad Norr Design, Minneapolis, Minnesota, and typeset by Toppan Best-set Premedia Limited. Printed and manufactured by Maple Press on acid-free paper.

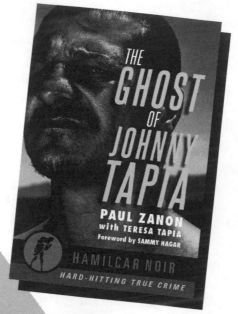

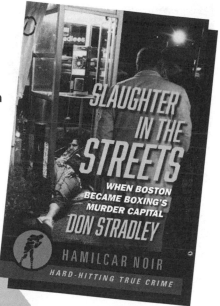

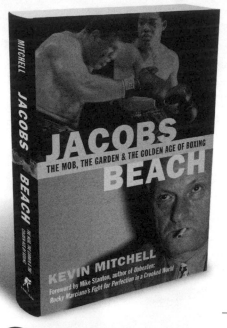

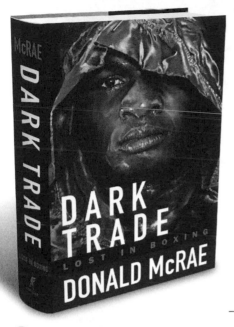

Over twenty years ago, Donald McRae set out across the United States and his adopted home, Britain, to find deeper meaning in the brutal trade that had transfixed him since he was a young man. The result is a stunning chronicle that captures not only McRae's compelling personal journey through the world of professional prizefighting, but also the stories of some of its biggest names—James Toney, Mike Tyson, Evander Holyfield, Oscar De La Hoya, Naseem Hamed, and others.

Singular in his ability to uncover the emotional forces that drive men to get into the ring, McRae brilliantly exposes the hopes and fears and obsessions of these legendary fighters, while revealing some of his own along the way. What he shares with them most, he comes to realize, is that he is hopelessly, and willingly, "lost in boxing."

In this new edition, released in the United States for the first time, and including a new chapter, it's clearer than ever why *Dark Trade* is considered one of the finest boxing books ever written.

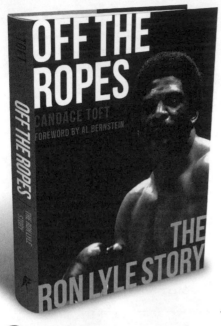
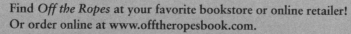